THE COMPLETE PARTY BOOK

THE

COMPLETE

PARTY

BOOK

How to Plan, Host, and Enjoy Your Party
from Conception to Conclusion

DON ERNSTEIN

with Deborah Sroloff

PHOTOGRAPHS BY DON ERNSTEIN

VIKING
STUDIO
BOOKS

To Larry Grusin;
You're right, I couldn't have done it without you!

VIKING STUDIO BOOKS
Published by the Penguin Group
Penguin Books USA Inc., 375 Hudson Street, New York, New York 10014, U.S.A.
Penguin Books Ltd, 27 Wrights Lane, London W8 5TZ, England
Penguin Books Australia Ltd, Ringwood, Victoria, Australia
Penguin Books Canada Ltd, 10 Alcorn Avenue, Toronto, Ontario, Canada M4V 3B2
Penguin Books (N.Z.) Ltd, 182–190 Wairau Road, Auckland 10, New Zealand

Penguin Books Ltd, Registered Offices: Harmondsworth, Middlesex, England

First published in 1994 by Viking Penguin, a division of Penguin Books USA Inc.

1 3 5 7 9 10 8 6 4 2

Photographs by Grey Crawford, pages 18 (top), 22 (top left, top right), 23 (bottom right), 27 (top and bottom),
30–31, 34, 50 (bottom), 55 (top), 59 (bottom), 62 (center, bottom left, bottom right), 66–67, 70–71,
74–75, 152–53, Copyright © Grey Crawford, 1994

LIBRARY OF CONGRESS CATALOGING-IN-PUBLICATION DATA
Ernstein, Don.
The complete party book: how to plan, host, and enjoy your party from conception to
conclusion / by Don Ernstein with Deborah Sroloff.
p. cm.
Includes index.
ISBN 0-670-84959-6
1. Entertaining. 1. Sroloff, Deborah. II. Title.
GV1471.E76 1994
793.2—dc 20 93-28131

Printed in Singapore
Set in Century Book Condensed and Gill Sans
Designed by Brian Mulligan

Acknowledgments

Whom do you thank and how do you thank them? In the process of completing a book, this seems to be the hardest part—to give credit where credit is due, and to be sure not to forget anyone.

First things first:

In my heart I know that my love and talent for entertaining, cooking, and eating was inherited from my grandmother Anna Ginsberg. It seemed as though food was served 'round the clock from her kitchen. Something was always going in or coming out of the oven. There was always much love that exuded from my "Bubbe," and she is in my heart forever.

These gifts that I inherited from her have kept me going for a long time.

In 1975, I met Bonnie Winston, who opened my eyes, my ears, and above all, my mouth to an even bigger world of food. We explored and experienced and shared, and became important friends. She's been an inspiration to me. I hope, perhaps, that I have been one to her, as well.

Through Bonnie I met Suzie Aron. Suzie has always been supportive of my abilities. When I started photographing my work to keep a record of what I'd done, she was the first to say, "There's a book here."

I owe my start as a professional caterer to Michele Andelson. She was having a brunch for 125 guests, and asked me to plan and cater it. She totally trusted me, and that brunch began my career.

Lilya Lekhgolts assists me in executing my parties; whether it's a dinner for 12 or for 1,000, she is there making sure that the food and quality are exactly what I want. She is my other self—I can't describe her any better. She makes my work fun. Her palette, eye, and sense of style are incomparable. And to Lana Margulyan, who, with Lilya, always stays until the job is done.

Jodie Evans and Max Palevsky have hired me to do many parties. From the first time we worked together, they understood my vision. Through them, I have met a diverse group of people who make up the entertainment and political tapestry of Los Angeles. They also introduced me to my agent, Ed Victor.

The experience of having Ed Victor as an agent has been one that I will always remember. Ed is supportive, immediately responsive, and a wonderful friend. He is always available for me. I look forward to working with him always!

Once my parties leave the kitchen and arrive at the party location, they come to life through the help of two special people, Rich Jones and Simonne Bogle. Through their knowledge I've learned so much. I love to put the finishing touches on my work, but I couldn't do it as comfortably without their hard work.

To realize lifelong dreams and ambitions is a concept I've always believed possible. My gifted dear friend Holly Hein showed me the way.

Thanks to Annie Gilbar for being instrumental in my book proposal.

Thanks to Deborah Sroloff, who put my thoughts and words in order. At Viking Studio Books, my editor, Martha Schueneman, and designer, Brian Mulligan, were instrumental in the content and design of this book. Thanks also to Barbara Williams and Neil Stuart, and to Michael Fragnito and Peter Mayer, who started the ball rolling.

Thanks to Grey Crawford for taking some of the photographs throughout the book.

Last but not least, I'd like to thank my parents, Grace and Dave Ernstein. They never discouraged me from expressing myself and my talents. I don't know whether they always understood the direction I was taking, but they never said no. I love you both.

FOR LENDING OBJECTS, KNOWLEDGE, AND SUPPORT

John & Pete's, Paulette Knight, Lillian Weirick, Cornucopia, Corinna Cotsen, Tobey Cotsen, Hallmark Cards, Crane & Co., Sweet Lady Jane, Classic Party Rentals, The Gifted Line, Cottura, Lucy Zahran, Sylvia Tidwell, Kathleen Brown, Cathy Unger, Beverly Thomas, Dee Sherwood, Hope Warschaw, Esther Wahl, and the staff of Wonderful Parties, Wonderful Foods.

Contents

Preface

I've produced thousands of parties. Some of them were for clients; others were my own. The one constant in every party is planning—the details to be dealt with, settings to be arranged, menus to be planned.

To my mind, the objective of a party should be to have fun. The main purpose of a party is to bring people together for a good time—and the host should have as good a time as the guests.

Throughout my career as a caterer, party planner, cook, host, and party-giver, I've become convinced that *anyone*, with the proper "tools of the trade," can give successful parties. By "tools" I don't mean pots and pans or spatulas or vases. I mean advice, hints, assistance, and a sense of confidence and joyousness in organizing, designing, and hosting parties.

I've been collecting books on entertaining, cooking, flower arranging, table setting, and other subjects related to entertaining and party giving for years. I purchase these books impulsively, because I'm always looking for that extra bit of advice, special recipe, or unusual, eye-catching, exceptional idea that will light up a party, give it zing, make it unforgettable.

But I've never found a single volume that encompasses all the information I believe is crucial to giving and enjoying a wonderful party. That book is what I've attempted to give you here.

I wrote this book to give you a step-by-step guide that will lead you through the planning and execution of your party. But even more than this, I want to emphasize that party giving itself can be a joyous, happy experience. We've all been to—or perhaps even hosted—parties where the hosts' nerves were so frazzled that by the time the party began, they couldn't wait for the event to end. Entertaining does not have to involve jittery nerves, or a quest for such perfection that all the fun, satisfaction, and humor go out of the process. Party giving can, and should be, every bit as much fun as partygoing.

In planning parties—my own and for my clients—I emphasize the element of fun. There has to be some spontaneity, even at the most assiduously, perfectly planned party. And when things go wrong, a sense of humor is invaluable to getting through any disaster. At one black-tie party I catered, the painstakingly assembled croquembouche collapsed in front of two hundred guests, then fell apart, with the pâte-à-choux balls rolling on the floor. It was a disaster, but I had to laugh at it. What else could I do?

I've been giving parties since I was twelve years old. One weekend when my parents went away, my sister and I invited eight friends over for a five o'clock sit-down dinner. Although I prepared a menu that my mother had served many times to her friends, I of course thought that my version was infinitely better. After all, I *was* almost thirteen! I served iceberg lettuce with bottled Italian dressing, a beef brisket that I sprinkled with dehydrated onion soup, wrapped in foil, and cooked in the oven, and a casserole of frozen vegetables (peas, I think) and canned soup with potato chips on top. The beverage was soda pop. For dessert, I proudly served a frozen lemon-meringue pie.

That was my first party.

I'm happy to say that I've come a long way since then. The menus are a little more sophisticated, wine and mineral water have replaced the pop, the vegetables are fresh—and there are no potato chips on top of them. One thing that hasn't changed, however, is that the parties I give today are just as wonderful emotionally as that first one was: the detail in the preparation is the same, the love that goes into the cooking is as deep, and the joy in sharing what I've planned and made is as splendid.

Wonderful Parties—that's what I believe in. Not perfect or magnificent or superb, but wonderful. To me, a wonderful party encompasses all those things and more. It means a feeling of joy in the delightful anticipation of planning a celebration—of happily designing and arranging and making a dream come true. It means beginning a process of heartwarming exhilaration that ends in a memorable sharing of your time and spirit with friends. Whether you choose to give a party that is modest or grand, for four or forty or four hundred, a small tea or a large wedding, you want it to be wonderful.

Wonderful parties should be a delight to plan and a joy to give. But it's important to remember that a wonderful party doesn't have to be perfect. In fact, an obsession with perfection can be the doom of a truly joyous party. A feeling of spontaneity must always be in the air. And though wonderful parties should be a delight and a joy, they aren't always. Too often, hosts get overwhelmed by the planning and by the sheer scope of all the details, even for the smallest of groups in the simplest of ways of entertaining. It doesn't have to be so. That's what this book is all about.

There's no denying that party giving takes planning, organization, and help. But it's very easy to make giving wonderful parties an exciting, inventive, and rewarding process to anticipate with pleasure rather than to dread. It can be very simple, and it can even be fun to plan and give wonderful parties.

The guidelines I suggest allow you the freedom to have the party you want. While it's an all-too-true irony that you spend far more time planning a party than you do hosting it, it is time well spent.

In this book, I intend to untangle all those mysteries and give you a foolproof guide for making a special event practically problem-free.

I share with you the elements that go into giving a wonderful party—one that will make you proud and that your friends will remember forever: from the unforgettable invitation that sets the tone, to creating the atmosphere, to planning the menu and designing the table, to selecting the flowers or making the centerpieces, to choosing the wines and serving the delicious foods.

I share with you some hard-earned advice—about working with a caterer; hiring extra help; creating an ideal atmosphere with lighting, music, and other elements; and dealing with party jitters. It's all here—everything you ever wanted to know about giving and enjoying wonderful parties. So, let the party begin!

THE COMPLETE PARTY BOOK

PART ONE

Party Basics

CHAPTER ONE

Planning Your Party

BEFORE YOU START: THE BASICS

Although parties come in myriad guises, they all share one trait: parties bring people together for a brief period of time to share food, drink, and conversation. Parties come in all different shapes, sizes, flavors, and rhythms. You can tailor a party to fit your personality and style, allowing you to entertain in a way that not only suits the occasion, but does so in a manner you are comfortable with. If, for example, you're a jeans and T-shirt type of person, you may feel that a black-tie wedding is not the way you want to go—and that's perfectly fine. Just because an occasion is fraught with certain preconceived notions, you shouldn't be afraid to alter traditions that you don't feel comfortable with.

After all, what's the point of giving a party if *you* won't have a good time?

Every successful party requires careful planning from the moment you first decide to throw it. Planning any party involves the same steps, whether it's a casual dinner for four or an all-out bash for hundreds.

If you take a cue from the basic rules of journalism, a good place for every party-giver to start is with a simple list: why, who, where, when, what, and how much? Answering these brief questions will provide a framework that will support your event and will simplify the process tremendously. "Why" will determine the reason or occasion for the party. "Who" will assemble your guest list. "Where" will choose the location; "when," the date and time. "What" will give you the nitty-gritty of the party. "How much" will give you a realistic budget to work with.

Why?

"Why am I having this party?" That's the fundamental question to address in planning your event, and the answer will shape the party. A party can simply be an organized excuse to bring a bunch of friends together for a casual, spontaneous dinner at home—say, to "christen" a new dining-room table. Or it may be for the traditional occasions we celebrate: a wedding reception, a birthday party, a landmark anniversary, or a housewarming. While most parties are, not surprisingly, centered on happy occasions, some are more solemn, such as a reception following a funeral. And still other get-togethers are of a busi-

ness nature, where your professional life will be mixed with pleasure. In short, there are as many different types of parties as there are events in everyday life—myriad and nearly infinite, each with its very own character.

Who?

The "why" of a party is instrumental in determining the "who." Weddings will most likely include a mix of family and friends, as will showers, birthdays, bar and bat mitzvahs, and christenings; a business-dinner guest list might include important clients and colleagues; while a cocktail party can bring old friends together or introduce people who have never met.

When compiling your guest list, keep in mind that the smaller the party, the more intimate it is. Because there's less margin for error, you'll want to choose your guests for smaller parties carefully. They don't necessarily need to know each other or have similar interests, but with just a few people around a dinner table, a contentious, ornery person could be a real sore thumb, whereas he or she would just be part of the "mix" at a larger party. Because a larger party allows for diversity in the guest list, you may want to save the more interesting or volatile combinations for a more populous event. Remember that putting the right people together is like chemistry—sometimes it's magic, and sometimes it's combustible!

Once you've finalized your list, write or type it in alphabetical order (if you have a computer, so much the better, as you can easily make any changes, and save it for future reference). This

Though the people make the party, sometimes the most assiduously chosen guest list can have a glitch or two. As a gracious and good host, you can provide the ambiance, food, and drink—but you can't make people have a good time. If you give a party that didn't go exactly the way you wanted it to, you can always give another one.

makes it easy to keep track of your RSVPs and to note any special needs a guest may have (an allergy to certain foods or to cigarette smoke, or a need to sit at the end of the table).

Where?

The next decision to make is "where?" Most of the time, your personality and lifestyle will automatically determine where your party should be. There are many possible party locations, both indoors and out, at home and away. There are also countless different ways to use them, in terms of seating, eating, and entertaining.

Some of the most creative parties are held in some of the most unusual locations—in the din-

ing area of an ethnic market (a friend once put on a fabulous birthday party in a Mexican *mercado*, where the cost of food was next to nothing and mariachis serenaded the group all night long, for only a few dollars in tips), or in a city park where you can barbecue up a storm without having to worry about cleaning the grill. Let your imagination run wild. The unexpected can be filled with the most fun.

When?

In general, the time of day you decide to hold your party and the type of food you serve will be intertwined, at least in the case of brunches, luncheons, dinner parties, and dessert parties.

Using your kitchen counter for a buffet is an unexpected surprise—unconventional settings are fun for casual parties.

Combining flowers, fruits, and vegetables makes for incredible centerpieces. Note that they are low so you can see over them.

Some of the accessories for a tea party—glasses, tea service, cups, and saucers—can be all set up prior to your party.

This holiday dessert buffet was strategically placed in front of this arched window. Setting the food in outstanding surroundings only makes it look more spectacular.

I'm a fan of dahlias; these are grown by Smoky Smith. When they are loosely arranged with burgundy, "plume-y" weeds, there's not much more you need on a table.

Pastel Luray buffet plates and serving bowls that continue the pink, blue, and yellow theme are perfect for a baby shower. The flowers are also soft and pastel. Beverages were served in baby bottles with straws, and the silver was wrapped in cloth diapers, which guests used as napkins.

An alphabetized printed list is invaluable for large parties at which gifts are involved, such as weddings, birthdays, and showers. Simply enter the gift received next to the guest's name—a small detail that greatly facilitates things when the time comes for writing thank-you notes.

Because weddings, showers, bar and bat mitzvahs, and birthday parties can take place at a variety of times, you'll want to choose what is best for you, your budget, and your guests. Here's a basic timetable:

Breakfast parties
before 11:00 A.M.
Brunch parties
between 10:00 A.M. and 2:00 P.M.
Lunch parties
between 11:30 A.M. and 2:30 P.M.
Tea parties
between 3:00 and 5:00 P.M.
Cocktail parties
between 6:00 and 8:00 P.M.
Dinner parties
between 7:00 and 9:00 P.M.
Dessert parties
from 9:00 P.M. on
Late-supper parties
from 10:00 P.M. on

✧   ✧   ✧

It's important to consider how the party you're giving will fit into the schedule of your guests. For people with small children who are dependent on babysitters, a very late event can be problematic. Weekend afternoons can be a great time for bringing together families.

Often a fine party can be built around an event like the Grammy Awards or the Oscars or the Super Bowl, when people get together to cheer on their favorites. If a party is for a very special event, like a decade birthday, not only is evening appropriate, but so is evening wear; there's something about dressy clothes that makes an ordinary event extraordinary.

How Much?

You don't have to spend a fortune to have a wonderful party. The most important aspect of creating a party budget is to set—and stick to—a realistic limit. Plan carefully for all your expenditures. Of course, as anyone who has ever given a party knows, it's not unusual for a budget to run over or expand right when you're in the middle of things. This generally happens when you've amended your original party plan or decided to add or change various details. At that point, you have the option: you can go for the extras or not. But by keeping the last-minute items down to a minimum and by following the guidelines in this section, you should be able to hew pretty closely to your projected party budget.

Remember to "pad" your budget, since emergencies can pop up—the cake you baked fell on the floor and you have to buy a new one at the bakery; the flowers you bought in the morning have all wilted because the house got too hot and you need to replace them.

First, prioritize where your dollars will be best spent, according to your strengths as a host and to satisfy the objectives you wish your party to accomplish. Make a list of expenditures—invitations, food, party favors, labor, flowers, candles or other decorations, entertainment, beverages, and rentals—and determine what you can afford for each. Whether you choose to prepare the food yourself or purchase it, for example, you'll need to decide how much you want to spend on it first. This is also the time to figure out where you can "cut corners": for instance, if you use flowers from your garden and arrange them yourself, you'll have money to hire a musician.

Even for a small dinner party, you may want a housekeeper or even just a student to assist with the setting up and cleaning up. For a larger party, you may need a bartender, waiters, and a clean-up crew.

GETTING THE HELP

Part of being a successful host is knowing your strengths and weaknesses. Are you an ace at planning, yet can't quite execute an event? Are you perfectly at ease whipping up a formal dinner for twenty, yet fall apart when it come time to serve it? You may want to consider hiring someone whose strengths complement your own.

To be able to be a guest at your own party (especially if it's particularly large or lavish) you may need some extra hands to check on the food, take guests' coats, make and freshen drinks, and so forth. Depending on your budget, there are a variety of ways to find help. It is best to rely on the recommendations of friends you trust in such matters, a professional staffing agency, your housekeeper, or a reliable, responsible student you know. The people you hire can assist you in preparing the party site, cooking and serving the food, and cleaning up. As a rule, a sit-down event will require more help in the kitchen and on the floor than a buffet.

When you are hiring additional staff, be sure to delineate their responsibilities. Outline exactly the type of party it is, what is to be served (and in what order), and how many guests will attend. If you're not providing uniforms, explain how you'd like the staff to dress. Stress to them that it is a party and that everyone should have fun, including the people working it, and that they should be pleasant, courteous, and helpful to your guests. The clearer and more specific you are about your wants and needs, the less the chance of mistakes, miscommunications, and slipups.

Orchids in old French apothecary bottle "vases" echo the china pattern. A vintage linen runner and napkins repeat the delicate cutout pattern on the dishes. A contemporary plastic napkin ring finishes the table. Mixing and matching is fun and results in unexpected pleasures.

Breakfast parties in this cozy nook are cheery. Sunflowers are favorites of mine; they're always smiling. Use the things you love; these Bauer plates come in all different colors, as do the bowls. By changing the plates around, the color scheme can change too!

Most people are so taken with the view they can't focus on the food. All of the elements came together for this noon wedding lunch.

Crudités for a crowd: This stationary appetizer setting can feed many guests and, positioned correctly, it's accessible from all sides. The crudités were all put on a table about 7 feet square, and the table was completely covered with food.

Weather permitting, outdoor dining is splendid. Dee Sherwood's enchanted garden, with all its mazes and living and dining areas, is one of my favorite party settings.

The kumquat motif on the plate is played up by real kumquats in the vase. Adding fruits and vegetables to the water in clear vases is lovely—and hides unsightly stems. Note the oversized two-sided place cards: guests can read the name from across the table.

Party Planning Checklist

Occasion:	*Jack's birthday*
Date:	October 3
Time:	*9:00 P.M.*
Place:	*our house*
Type of party:	*dessert buffet*
Guest count:	*36*
Budget:	*moderate*
Invitations:	*from card shop*
RSVP date:	*by telephone 10 days before*
Food:	*buy 5 desserts, make 2*
Beverages:	*coffee, decaf coffee, tea, champagne, and dessert wine*
Tableware:	*white linen napkins and tablecloths; clear glass dishes and glassware*
Rentals:	*55-cup coffeemaker, 24 champagne flutes, 6 chairs*
Flowers:	*order centerpiece*
Music:	*a pianist at my piano*
Lighting:	*use all candlesticks; make sure dimmers work*
Photographer/Video:	*get film for camera*
Entertainment:	*none*
Valet parking:	*none*
Extra help:	*2—one bartender, one server*
Caterer:	*none*

Party Planning Checklist

Occasion:

Date:

Time:

Place:

Type of party:

Guest count:

Budget:

Invitations:

RSVP date:

Food:

Beverages:

Tableware:

Rentals:

Flowers:

Music:

Lighting:

Photographer/Video:

Entertainment:

Valet parking:

Extra help:

Caterer:

CHAPTER TWO

Invitations

I love invitations. In fact, for me, the invitation itself is often as important as the actual event. Besides providing a first impression, the invitation sets the tone for what's to come. It's rare that a spectacular invitation is followed by a lackluster party.

There are as many ways of extending invitations as there are types of parties. Although there are some guidelines for tailoring the invitation to the party, it's mostly a matter of common sense: You'd never send formal, engraved invitations to a casual backyard get-together, or invite people just a week in advance by telephone to a black-tie wedding. The basic rule is to craft the invitation to fit the event.

While invitations can be extended either well in advance or spontaneously, you should keep in mind that people's schedules tend to become more and more crowded the longer you wait. For a small, intimate dinner, asking guests by telephone is perfectly acceptable. Because you want to be sure you don't forget to mention any important details, make a checklist of the information you need to convey to your guests: the date, time, occasion, mode of dress, place, and your phone number. Be sure to mention whether the event is to be held inside or outdoors. If you're hosting a dinner party, let guests know whether you'll serve cocktails beforehand or if dinner is to be served promptly. Walking into a party can sometimes be overwhelming for a guest, and an invitation that gives all the details in a clear, kind way makes all the difference in helping everyone feel comfortable.

Perhaps the most essential detail—especially if your guests may be leaving a message on an answering machine—is to ask them to RSVP by a specific date. If any guests haven't responded to your invitation by that time, feel free to call and gently inquire if they'll be able to attend. When the RSVPs do start coming in, keep track of them by checking off who has said yes or no on your printed guest list. If you've had a cancellation for a less formal event, it's all right to invite another guest up to the day of the party—but only if you're sure that person won't be offended by a last-minute invite. Do be honest, and don't make up a story about an impromptu get-together—the truth always seems to come out!

Invitations for a very formal event, such as a wedding, bar or bat mitzvah, or anniversary party, should be sent out six to eight weeks prior to the event. Invitations for a large but less formal party, such as a birthday, should be sent out four weeks in advance. Don't forget to leave extra time—up to a month—for ordering and printing custom invitations.

Written Invitations

Written invitations come in an almost endless variety: from a packet of simple preprinted fill-in cards found in a drugstore, to the most elegant engraved, foil-stamped, multisheet invitations created by a custom invitation shop or fine stationer.

The fabulous selection of preprinted invitations found in commercial card shops covers the spectrum of party needs, and most are not very costly. They come in a variety of sizes, designs, and colors to suit your style and fit the theme of your party. Some are serious, others are whimsical. Some card shops offer in-house printing that's quite affordable, and some stores also provide sample books from which you can order custom invitations.

If you wish, there are many ways to personalize store-bought invitations. Customize them with calligraphic pen work, metallic inks, fancy stickers, rubber stamps, or sealing wax, or go to an art-supply store, specialty paper shop, or stationer to find papers, envelopes, or other novelty items that you can transform into wonderful invitations.

If your budget allows, there are specialty stationery and party shops, as well as professional party planners, that can create printed invitations to suit you and your event. Their prices are higher than a commercial card shop's, but it may be worth it to you to create a first impression that will be extra special. Specialty stores also often have calligraphy machines or calligraphers on staff to address the envelopes. Print and xerography shops offer same-day and 24-hour turn-around and color photocopying, as well as standard printing services.

The most memorable invitations are often the ones you make yourself. If you're so inclined and have the time, your guests will notice and appreciate this special touch. With beautiful papers and envelopes from a stationery or art-supply store, and a handwritten message in a metallic ink or calligraphic pen, making your own invitations needn't be a production. Card shops also sell beautiful blank cards that you can hand-letter or have printed. And don't forget that using rubber stamps, stickers, or your own original artwork is another effective option.

Sometimes a really special occasion warrants a truly special invitation—in either its design or its presentation. For one party, I stained heart-shaped wooden boxes (available at craft stores) green, glued on floral stickers, and decorated them with a gold pen (see step-by-step photographs on page 31). You can send a scroll tied with a ribbon. Such three-dimensional invitations will call for a different type of packaging—an unusually shaped envelope or a box that has to be hand-delivered—so keep in mind that it can be costly to send them.

When it comes to mailing more standard invitations, the post office has a terrific selection of colorful and beautifully designed commemorative stamps that can continue the theme of the invitation itself. Running invitations through a postage machine may be faster and more convenient, but it lacks an intimate feeling. It takes a little more time to add these personal touches, but it's worth it.

Electronic Invitations

Since this is the age of instant communication, what with stationary and cellular phones, personal computers with modems, and fax machines, you can also relay an invitation electronically. The same guidelines for written invitations apply to electronic ones.

Faxes are a fun and immediate way to reach someone. Some of your guests' fax machines may be in public or common areas, so if you fax an invitation to someone's office, be sensitive to the possibility of others you may know seeing it and feeling left out.

There's a rubber stamp to fit every occasion, and a different color or metallic ink to match it. You can go for cute or dramatic, and this is an inexpensive way to create great-looking invitations.

Packaged cards like these, courtesy of Crane & Co., come in all different designs and formats. Commemorative stamps and sealing wax add a special touch.

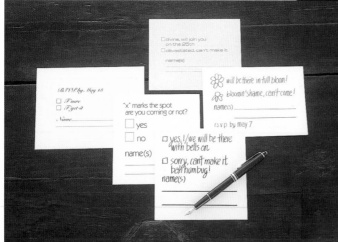

RSVP cards needn't be drab, especially if you personalize them to fit the theme of the invitation. Your guests will enjoy the element of fun.

Card shops have a variety of affordable, pre-packaged invitations, like these from Hallmark, or use blank cards and fill in the pertinent information yourself. Some stores offer on-the-spot service, where blank cards are custom printed with your message while you wait.

Michele Andelson is passionate about roses. For her fortieth birthday these heart-shaped boxes contained the invitations. They're quite easy to put together, and they're one of a kind. Here's how to do it:

1. First, paint the heart-shaped boxes (available at craft shops) inside and out with a green acrylic paint that's been thinned with water. Wait until they're completely dry before you go to the next step.

2. Apply rose stickers in all different sizes and colors to the boxes. You can decorate the boxes the same, or make each one different; suit yourself.

3. Using a metallic gold pen, outline the stickers and embellish the edges and sides of each box with patterns. This gives a finished look to the stickers and a fanciful look to the box.

4. To continue the rose theme, fill the box halfway with rose buds or your favorite potpourri.

5. Cut the invitations out of heavy paper; they should be slightly smaller than the inside of the box. Inscribe one side with a whimsical message, the other with the details. Put it and the RSVP card in the box. Now the box can be packaged for delivery to guests.

6. We packaged each heart box in a white box with tissue, and then wrapped it with a green gauze ribbon and an organdy floral ribbon. The boxes were then hand-delivered to each guest.

The Importance of RSVPs

The term "RSVP" comes from the French "répondez, s'il vous plaît," which means "please respond."

"Regrets only" as a form of RSVPs really doesn't work; most prospective guests won't even bother. Rather, make sure to specify a date for guests to RSVP by—at least one week before a casual event, at least two for a formal, catered affair—to avoid an avalanche of last-minute acceptances or regrets. Most caterers and bakers can change orders up to a few days before an event, but it's always nice to know how many guests to expect as far in advance as possible.

If you are sending an RSVP card along with the invitation, write a number on the back of each one. That number will correspond with each name on your list, in case the respondee forgets to fill out the card, as sometimes happens.

An invitation is the first communication between host and guest. A great invitation should get you really excited about the event to come; it alone will make you want to go.

CHAPTER THREE

Setting the Stage

I f the invitation is the cornerstone of a party, then the location is the party's foundation. It sets the stage and is greatly responsible for the mood and flow of a party. The place you choose to give a party makes a statement: it can be a very personal or a very grand one. Determining what you want your event to "say" depends largely on where it is held.

Home is where most parties take place, and there are many different ways to do a party at home. But don't forget about other locations—a hotel, a public or private garden, a church or synagogue, a club, a park, a historical site, a beach, or even someone else's home.

A tip for assembling seating arrangements if you're using assigned seats with place cards: on a piece of paper, draw circles or rectangles representing the number of tables you'll have. Write out your guests' names on individual strips of paper and place them on the circles or rectangles, moving them around until you get the mix that works best.

This sunny, airy room is perfect for breakfasts and small brunches and luncheons. The pine table is homey and casual, as are the sunflowers. Note that the green-and-yellow color scheme continues to the serving bowls in the wall recess.

Al fresco dining often means more dramatic settings than indoors; keep settings stark and simple to give the suroundings even more impact. As the light fades, the hurricane lamp will add glow.

Silver champagne buckets filled with red and lavender roses add a formal note and contrast with blooming red rose bushes in burlap sleeves.

For a large holiday party, this living room became the dining room. All the furniture was removed and stored in the garage. Rented tables, chairs, and linens, along with garlands, centerpieces, and lots of candles, make this room work. Round tables facilitate conversation and help keep a party festive.

If you are unsure how many tables and chairs will comfortably fit into a given space, and if the guest list starts to grow beyond your original plan, don't hesitate to call a party rental company for help with the logistics. They will not only be able to provide the extra tables, chairs, and other components you may need, but will also assist you with the floor plan and flow of the seating and guests.

PARTIES AT HOME

Home is where the heart *and* the hearth are, and if you love to cook, or simply enjoy sharing your place with others, that's probably where you'll choose to entertain most often. Even the smallest house or apartment can be the perfect backdrop for your event, as long as you tailor the flow of guests and the food and drink to the location.

A party at home is the most personal way to entertain. By inviting people into your home, you're asking them to come into your world, which is an extension of yourself. Whether you prepare the food yourself or have the party catered, it's still your home.

When you entertain at home, bring out your heirlooms or the collectibles you've been saving for a special occasion—*this* is that occasion! The things you've collected, whether vintage American pottery dishes, cake stands, or the family silver, say a lot about you and help to lend a personal touch. And don't be afraid to be original.

The following are some basic at-home party "floor plans":

⬦ *Use your dining room for a sit-down dinner.*

⬦ *Use another room in the house as an unexpected party space.*

⬦ *Do a stand-up cocktail or buffet party if there are too many people to seat.*

⬦ *Have the party flow indoors and outdoors.*

⬦ *Have the party outdoors only.*

Traffic and seating are very important elements of any party. If the party is a buffet or stand-up event, you don't want people crammed together in one big knot or standing in line waiting to get food. If possible, it is best in a buffet situation to position the serving tables in the center of the room, so that people can serve themselves from both sides. However, if space constraints preclude this, simply make the best of the space you have. But do try to walk through the buffet beforehand, so you can feel the flow in the room and get a sense of what positioning works and what doesn't work.

For larger parties, round tables seating six to eight people work best for facilitating the flow of conversation. Try to avoid using long tables, as you can only really talk to the person directly across from you or those on either side. A seating arrangement involving long tables usually feels more formal, too.

Another alternative, if you don't have enough seating to accommodate all the guests you wish to invite, or if the space you have for a party doesn't allow for everyone to be seated comfortably, is to have a party where your guests are standing, like a cocktail party, open house, or dessert party. For a stand-up party, finger food (food that doesn't need to be cut), either passed on trays or laid out on easily accessible buffet tables, coffee or end tables, or even countertops, is mandatory. And even though your party may be stand-up, you'll still need to have seating available. Supplement whatever seating is already in the room with extra chairs, cushions, or large throw pillows. Stair steps also work just fine as a place for guests to perch themselves.

If the weather permits, having the party flow from indoors to out can work beautifully, or you may choose to use your outdoor space exclusively.

When giving a party outdoors, be sure to specify that fact on the invitation, so guests will know to dress accordingly. Also, make sure that you have adequate heating and lighting. You may decide to have your outdoor party during the day, when dropping temperatures and darkening skies aren't really issues. And don't forget to cut the grass, spray for bugs, and water before that day.

If your party is to be held indoors, make sure that the space can comfortably accommodate the number of people you're inviting. If your dining-room table isn't big enough to seat everyone, then do a buffet with "fork food," where one utensil will suffice for eating the various dishes you serve (no guest should have to perform a juggling act at your party!).

If space is tight in the room or area where you want your guests to congregate, set up "mini-buffets" in different areas or rooms so that the flow works better and people aren't uncomfortably crowded together. For instance, if the party will take place mostly in your living room, set up various food "stations" in the kitchen and dining area as well as in the living room. It's good to keep in mind that guests tend to mass around the food, so you may want to serve the beverages in one place, the food in another, and desserts and coffee in yet another, just to keep the flow going smoothly.

Another option is to use someone else's home for your party, if you don't feel that yours is appropriate or spacious enough to accommodate the number of people you wish to invite, yet you wish to retain the personal touch a party given at home lends. In using a friend's or relative's home, you must take extra-special care to make sure that the preparation process isn't too disruptive to the home's owners and that, of course, when the party is over, the relationship isn't.

The glass containers holding the flowers were specially hand-painted by Sylvia Tidwell, a Los Angeles–based florist, with a leaf pattern to incorporate the tablecloth design. Oversized place cards are easy for guests to read, and the rose color matches the napkins.

Lynnie Cohen wanted to use three different sets of china for her party. I pulled it all together with a black-and-white taffeta plaid overlay, black-and-white polka-dot napkins, and all-white flowers.

Considering your guests' comfort is always important. Because most guests at this wedding, held at an out-of-the-way ranch, had to drive for about an hour to get to the location, we set up a lemonade stand, so a cool glass of lemonade and heart-shaped poppy-seed shortbread were waiting for them.

This afternoon party was given in the lovely but still rather generic party room of a condominium complex. A long, lavish display of flowers and food dressed up the drab surroundings.

Ceramic squash and eggplant salt and pepper shakers, along with the cabbage-leaf bowl for condiments, look as though they fell out of the centerpiece.

The beginnings of an outdoor party buffet setup. The garden makes such a strong statement that all the other elements— sold-color terra-cotta tablecloths, clear glass plates—need to complement the surroundings.

If you're giving a dinner party for twenty-four people, yet you don't have a complete dinner service for that many, don't hesitate to mix and match dishes, silver, or glassware. On the other hand, you may decide that you want to rent the components. Remember that most party rental companies have everything you need, from kitchen equipment to champagne flutes.

Also feel free to express yourself with favorite objects such as centerpieces or table accessories—candles in different-sized holders massed together, flowers freshly cut from the garden, pots of herbs, or anything that's a display of the things you love. However, remember that accessories are just that. They shouldn't overwhelm the food or the room or the host; they are meant to enhance, not camouflage.

PARTIES OUTSIDE THE HOME

If you choose to give your party outside the home, you have a spectrum of locations to select from. Some of the most common are restaurants and hotels, but a variety of public and private spaces may suit your needs as well.

Restaurants

A party in a restaurant is an entirely different experience from one you give in your home, simply because there are so many more elements and people involved, and you alone are not completely in control.

Many restaurants have private rooms to rent for parties of a variety of sizes. It's best to choose a favorite restaurant that you know and trust—that way you'll have a good idea what to expect, and they'll have a vested interest in making sure you're satisfied.

Communication is vital: make sure to discuss thoroughly with the restaurant what your needs and objectives are. Be sure to get in writing exactly what is included in the price they quote you, so that you don't get stuck with a bill studded with "extras." You'll want to know what kind of linens and tableware they're going to use to help make the space look festive. Can they take care of the flowers and centerpieces, and, if so, what will they look like (and will you be paying a premium for the convenience)? Remember that you are both client and boss here, so the restaurant should be willing to accommodate you (of course, within reason).

When you are choosing the menu, ask which dishes work best prepared for a group. If you have a favorite dish that doesn't appear on the menu, don't hesitate to ask if the kitchen is able to prepare it. And if you have any guests with special dietary needs, be sure to inquire whether those needs can be met. Once you've chosen the menu, be sure to sample all the dishes.

Also discuss the lighting and whether any background music will be played (or if you can bring your own). A very important consideration is the number of staff members who will be tending your event; you'll want to make sure that there will be an appropriate amount of service available.

Hotels

Many hotels have banquet rooms or gardens that are used for parties, as well as a banquet or food-and-beverage manager to help you plan yours. Ask if you can peek in on a party being held at the hotel in order to see how the room you'd like to use looks all done up—preferably at the time of day or evening you're going to have your party.

Watch out for hidden costs, and find out up front exactly what details are and aren't included in the price you are quoted. At many hotels, everything is charged separately: drinks, hors d'oeuvres, food, service, parking, special linens and tableware, tax and tip, and even cake-cutting fees.

At the same time, be sure to find out what extras the hotel will be willing to include or throw in; sometimes, if you don't ask, you don't get. Do they have beautiful candelabra or centerpieces that are part of the deal? Remember that hotels are part of the service industry, and they are set up to take care of you. As with a restaurant, you

A late-afternoon wedding was set at a ranch. The wedding arch was designed to look natural and blends into the site. In contrast, the guests wore black tie.

Patios and gardens at private homes or rented public spaces offer unlimited possibilities for entertaining. On this particular property, five areas, each with distinct foliage, had room for guest seating and food and beverage service. Remember not to water the day of your party, or to spray for bugs, and to turn off automatic sprinklers.

Everything is set and ready to go for tea in the garden; the food will be brought out just before serving. With this spectacular garden, simple potted plants on the table and the buffets are all you need.

Party setups, like arranging chairs for a pre-dinner presentation, must be considered when choosing a location. After the presentation, staff placed the chairs around the dining tables, which were in another area.

This rented oceanside property was a magnificent site for a wedding, but was not without logistical problems. Everything had to be brought in—tables, chairs, linens, dance floor, heaters, lamps, and kitchen facilities, for starters.

If you don't feel comfortable with the location itself or with the people you're dealing with, it may be best to continue your search. A site that's fraught with too many restrictions, or a staff who can't provide you with the caliber of service you desire, cannot make up for a great view or beautiful decor.

are simply bringing a business more business in the form of your guests. Hotels need you, too.

Make sure to ask about time constraints. If there is another event immediately following yours, you'll have to clear out your party by a certain hour. Also, as with restaurants, make sure to sample the food.

Rented or Public Spaces

You can really give your imagination and creativity free rein should you decide to use a unique rented space for your party. An artist's loft, an airplane hangar, or a botanical garden are just a few of the out-of-the-ordinary spaces that can transform a good party into a truly magical one. Decide whether you would like your event to be inside or outdoors, and proceed from there. For ideas, you can consult guidebooks, the chamber of commerce, rental companies, caterers, party planners, friends, historical societies, and parks and recreation offices. In fact, you'll probably be pleasantly surprised at the variety of party-friendly locations you'll find.

Parties held in rented or public spaces may have a different set of details to checklist from parties held at home or in a restaurant or hotel. Be sure to inquire about any restrictions involving the number of people you're allowed to host, noise levels, music, the serving of alcoholic beverages, parking, and the time frame. Other things you will need to know include whether a special permit is required, if rental of the party space covers insurance or liability, and what the rental fee is. If the space is a public park or other common space,

Don't be afraid to ask a lot of questions; while parties

may be everyday occurrences for a hotel, your party

is the only one you should be concerned with,

and you have every right to make sure

that you get the party you want.

find out what security and restroom facilities are available, how far in advance you need to reserve it, and how private it is. If you will be unnerved by uninvited passers-by meandering through your party at a beautiful garden park with a lake, it may be wise to find another location.

The facilities you choose will likely dictate what type of food will work best. If there is no kitchen or other appropriate food-preparation area, you'll have to plan accordingly. If you want to barbecue or grill, find out what cooking apparatus is available, and if none is, whether you can bring your own. If your event requires electricity and running water for lighting, music, or food preparation, make sure that there are convenient, accessible outlets and taps.

For an outdoor event, find out if you'll need to enclose, tent, or partially screen the space. Be sure to visit the site at the time of day you're planning to give your party. If, for example, you are hosting an afternoon tea at a botanical garden, check to see if the sun will be beating down on guests' heads; if so, arrange for umbrellas to shade them. You'll also want to ensure that the ground or lawn won't be muddy or wet, that sprinklers won't go off in the middle of your party, and that there are adequate restroom and parking facilities. In case of rain, cold, or other elements, have an alternative venue lined up.

While a party in a rented space may require coordinating more elements than in other locations, a wedding at a historic mansion or a child's fantasy party at a beautiful public zoo can be an event that your guests will always remember.

CHAPTER FOUR

Food

Food plays a starring role at parties. More than mere nourishment, it's both a conversation piece and an art form. Good food is sensuous in that it enlists all the senses—not only taste and smell, but color and texture. When you plan a menu, all these elements should be taken into consideration.

When planning your menu, also consider the dietary restrictions of your guests. These days, it's very likely that at least some will be vegetarian, or have some health or dietary restriction. Therefore, it's a good idea, especially for small dinner parties, to find out beforehand if any of your guests have particular foods that they can't or won't eat. While this certainly doesn't mean that you have to make a separate menu for each guest, be prepared; have enough in the way of side dishes, or perhaps another entree as an alternative, so that they can still feel a part of the party. Be sure to offer nonalcoholic drinks to accommodate those who don't partake of spirits.

A real party "don't" is running out of food in the middle of an event; you *never* want that to happen. Don't prepare just enough for one serving for each person. You don't necessarily have to double everything, but some guests may want seconds, and most will want to taste a little of everything. Even people who are normally very circumspect about what and how much they eat often throw caution to the winds at a party.

At the same time, you don't want to overfeed your guests. If you're giving a dinner party, it isn't necessary to serve a lot of hors d'oeuvres. In fact, people are usually so hungry by the time they get to a party that they tend to overindulge on predinner nibbles, which renders them stuffed by the time the meal is served. Something as simple as nuts you've roasted or tasty olives offered with before-dinner drinks will suffice.

A good rule of thumb is to figure one and a half portions per person of everything you plan to serve. It's nice to have something left over for the next day; often, the host hardly gets a chance to eat at his or her own party, and you probably won't want to cook, anyway. This rule should also help you calculate the potential food costs.

WHO IS GOING TO PREPARE THE FOOD?

You have many options as to how to do the food at your party: you can prepare it yourself, buy take-out, hire a caterer, do a potluck dinner with friends—the only limit is your own imagination and how much work you're willing to invest.

Another factor in calculating food costs is determining who will prepare it. Don't assume that doing it yourself is always the most economical route—it can often cost more than prepared or even catered food, especially if you consider the value of your time.

If you do decide to prepare the food yourself, do it only if you enjoy the cooking and preparation involved. If you're not at ease in the land of pots and pans yet find yourself elbow-deep in them, there's a good chance that you'll be the person who has the worst time at his own party. Know your limitations as a host, and work within them. There's nothing wrong with using prepared or take-out foods.

Many restaurants will be happy to prepare food to go, so you may want to ask them to send you a menu. Gourmet markets with take-out counters often supply brochures or handouts listing the items they offer. Whenever possible, let your fingers do the walking. Call the markets, restaurants, or purveyors you plan to use to find out the prices of the items you want, how far in advance they need to be picked up, or if they can be delivered (and if there's a delivery fee).

Home Made

Get ideas from food magazines or favorite cookbooks, and use them as resources to create your own menus. Mix and match elements, including recipes that you've collected or devised yourself, or have guests bring different courses.

Don't hesitate to ask for recipes of dishes you particularly enjoy from a favorite restaurant or a friend. People are usually flattered by such requests and happy to share—though some cooks occasionally "forget" a secret ingredient, so your version may not be the same.

Potluck parties are a fun option, since everyone gets to participate and become a part of the party. All you as host have to do is orchestrate who brings what and take care of the background details. The problem that most commonly arises at potluck parties is an overlap of dishes. Make sure each guest has been assigned a specific dish, and keep careful track of who's bringing what.

You Don't Have to Make It Yourself to Call It Your Own!

If you don't have the inclination or time to do all the work yourself, you may wish to supplement your menu with take-out food. A wealth of possibilities exists—restaurants, gourmet shops, and specialty markets. You might even find terrific ready-made foods at the deli counter of a major supermarket.

If I have a motto as a party-giver, it is "You don't have to make it yourself to call it your own." Even the busiest people can entertain with relative ease, in ways that suit their style, taste, budget, and schedule, by taking advantage of the wealth of take-out food. This is the perfect solution for those who want to give parties (or *have* to, for business or social purposes), but have neither the time nor the inclination to do all the shopping and preparation necessary, yet don't want to hire a caterer. You can put together a wonderful menu by letting your fingers do the walking and picking up—or having delivered—your party-to-go.

Most restaurants, from the smallest mom-and-pop joint to the most upscale eatery, will package food to go.

Although you can get practically anything to go, certain cuisines lend themselves more readily to take-out: Chinese, Italian, Japanese, Mexican, Indian, Middle Eastern, and Thai work particularly well. Ask the restaurant which dishes travel best, what needs to be reheated and how, and what should be refrigerated. When taking out from a market, make sure that the food tastes as good as it looks—be sure to sample before you buy.

Many supermarkets boast international cheese and deli departments along with in-store rotisseries; in some parts of the country, you'll even find sushi counters and a sophisticated selection of wines and beers. At ethnic markets you can get all sorts of exotic and delicious dishes to go. Explore and enjoy!

A little-known fact is that you can usually order selected dishes from a professional caterer and pick them up—you don't have to have your entire party catered.

If you prefer, mix and match: get appetizers from a Middle Eastern market, the main course from a gourmet deli, and dessert from your favorite bakery.

Ask if you can bring your own serving platters, bowls, baskets, and other party pieces to restau-

During the summer and early fall months, local farmer's markets are usually full of wonderful fruits and vegetables. These beautiful tomatoes need only be washed, sliced, and tossed with a little fresh basil, salt, and pepper. Arrange squashes in baskets or bowls for a vegetable centerpiece, then cook them *after* your party!

It takes certain skills to cook Chinese food; I always rely on wonderful take-out resources, but transfer the food to my platters and bowls. I rolled the chopsticks in napkins (forks were nearby), and extra, empty take-out containers were used as plates.

Right: One hazard of outdoor parties: uninvited "guests." Oscar was close to devouring this mascarpone and prosciutto torta, served with herbed toast rounds. *Below:* For large gatherings—and large buffets—I sometimes label the food. Guests then know exactly what you're serving. For this tea party, the sandwich fillings were described. *Below right:* Cool hues of green and white were the color scheme at this luncheon; the food blends in. The silver, wrapped in napkins, is at the end of the buffet, so guests don't have to perform a juggling act.

rants, delis, or markets and have the food placed on them to save you from having to return borrowed items.

One of the best parties I've done was one at which we served Chinese take-out. We got extra containers from the restaurant—the traditional white cardboard take-out models; the food was transferred onto platters, and everyone used the containers as their "plates." It was great fun, the guests all got a kick out of this novel presentation, and it was the easiest thing in the world. "Fun" should be the operative word whenever you entertain; it is the very essence of entertaining. That, and people getting together to share good food and a good time.

USING A CATERER

In many endeavors—painting a house, fixing a car, planting a tree—sometimes it is best to call in a professional. Some people are born to entertain, others learn how to do so with aplomb, and still others discover that hiring a pro to put on their parties is the way to go. If a party starts to get too big or too elaborate for you to comfortably handle on your own, even if you're an inveterate party-giver, or if the occasion is so special that you want someone else to take care of the big and small details and coordinate them all, you may want to call upon the expertise of a caterer who can put your event together for you, from the invitations to the final clean-up.

Caterers are a sort of party conjurer; they will work with you every step of the way in planning and executing your event. Once you have established your budget, contact a few prospective caterers and ask them to meet you at your party site (if a caterer tells you that that isn't necessary,

let it be a red flag—*don't* hire that person). A good caterer will be happy to meet with a potential client, will have a portfolio of past events he or she has done, and can act as a party planner taking care of invitations, rentals, decorations, staffing, entertainment, valet parking, and more, as well as the menu.

A caveat here if you plan to have a restaurant "cater" your event: some restaurants may claim that they cater parties, but this isn't always the same as a full-service caterer. A restaurant generally isn't used to working "off-campus," whereas a caterer is used to taking the show on the road. A caterer will not just provide and cook the food, but will take care of everything. This isn't to say that no restaurants can provide this service; just check into their work very carefully.

How Do I Find a Good Caterer?

To find a good, responsible caterer, think of a party you attended that was particularly well executed, or ask friends for recommendations. If hiring someone sight unseen out of the phone book is your only resource, be sure to interview at least three different caterers, attend events they are putting on, and, above all, taste their food.

When you first meet with a caterer, it is very important for you to go over any of your personal likes and dislikes and to be very clear about exactly what you expect of the caterer and his or her staff, as well as what you wish to accomplish with your event.

Rather than having prospective caterers prepare a tasting menu for you, it is preferable to attend their actual events if possible. You'll get a better feel for the caterer's work if you sample it on location.

Although catering is often thought of as a luxury, it doesn't have to be expensive; in fact, for some parties, especially larger ones, it may be more cost-effective to hire a caterer. However, catering *is* a luxury in the sense that the caterer is providing a service, and you should feel pampered and in good, capable hands. Hosts of catered affairs should be able to feel like guests at their own parties.

In the excitement of planning an event, you may forget one imperative detail. Make sure that the caterer you hire is running a legal, aboveboard operation and is in possession of any and all necessary licenses (such as one for reselling alcohol, if the caterer is selling you liquor), bonds, and insurance and workers' compensation for its employees. You should have a contract covering the services provided. This is very, very important, because if your caterer isn't protected, you'll be the liable party if something goes wrong. A reputable caterer, running a legitimate business, will welcome you to see their kitchen. A full-service caterer will also be able to take care of any last-minute emergencies.

Although many caterers may not necessarily be on hand for the entire party, make sure he or she is there for at least part of it. If the caterer has a crackerjack organized staff of regulars, it is not imperative that he or she stay the length of the event. If a party is well planned, it should be able to "unfold" without the caterer, but a good one will at least want to survey the field personally, and it certainly makes you as a host feel more secure. A caterer should arrive about two hours before the party is to begin, with the crew, to oversee and take part in the setup; it is incredibly exciting to see an empty room that looks like nothing go

through a Cinderella-like transformation. And if a couple of guests wander in a half hour early, the caterer will be there, ready to serve them a drink and offer them an hors d'oeuvre.

It is vital to select someone you feel completely comfortable with, whom you trust to coordinate all aspects of your event, someone you are not intimidated by (and who is not intimidated by you). You want a caterer with high energy, not high anxiety. You should feel cared for and special throughout the entire process. Your party may be the tenth one your caterer has worked on that week, but a professional will make you feel as though yours is the *only* one, and that you are getting absolutely all the attention you deserve (and paid for!).

BEVERAGES

That timeless credo for parties—eat, drink, and be merry—still holds true, yet many hosts often don't think about the "drink" part of the equation until the day of the party. Planning and purchasing beverages is one detail that can be taken care of as soon as you've decided upon a menu. On page 57 is a chart that will help you determine how much liquor, mixers, and soft drinks you should have on hand. Don't forget to take inventory of what you already have before you go shopping. You don't want to end up buying rarely used items like grenadine or bitters when you have full bottles of them in your liquor cabinet.

Below: Full-blown garden roses and a vintage rose-patterned tablecloth from my collection are the perfect foil for these two desserts, which were very small and were nestled in around the flowers.

Top right: Figs are such a beautiful fruit that, when they are in season, they frequently appear on party menus. Cutting them in half and piping with a little goat cheese is a simple yet stunning way to present them. Make sure the figs are ripe but not mushy.

Center right: Artichokes are another beautiful food. These are stuffed with garlic and fresh herbs, and will be steamed in a seasoned broth.

Bottom right: English summer puddings are filled with strawberries and garnished with edible sweetheart roses. If you're using edible flowers, make sure they're unsprayed and not chemically treated.

For a cocktail party, put the bar on a table in the living room to take advantage of other areas in your home. Experiment! Place other food stations on surfaces through the party space.

Right: Lace-trimmed napkins lining the baskets and a cherub tied on gossamer ribbon around the neck of this vase full of baby's breath are soft touches for a baby shower–tea.

Below: When you set up your buffet, make sure it's accessible on both sides. This way, there never appears to be a long line. Guests can walk around the table and take samples of everything.

Choosing Wines

When buying wine, particularly of a vineyard, type, or vintage you aren't familiar with, buy a bottle to sample before you serve it to your guests. If you have a relationship with a wine merchant, or if you particularly trust a salesperson at a liquor store, or even have a friend who's an oenophile, ask his or her advice. A reputable merchant will also help you figure out how much you'll need and should take back unopened bottles— but be sure to check on the return policy before buying. (A hint: if you plan to ice the wine in buckets, wrap each bottle in a plastic bag to keep the label from getting wet and sliding off. Any unopened bottles will be intact should you need to return them.) Often, merchants will deliver larger orders, including ice and mixers, with the bottles already chilled.

Spirited Drinks Without Alcohol

It certainly isn't mandatory that you serve a full bar, or any hard liquor at all; serving just wine, champagne, and, for certain foods, beer is perfectly fine. Not every guest will drink alcohol, and among those who do, some drink only beer and wine. Always have some nonalcoholic drinks, especially mineral waters (both still and bubbly), on hand. Many nonalcoholic beers, wines, and sparkling wines are now widely available; they taste wonderful, contain fewer calories than their alcoholic counterparts, and are a thoughtful addition to your bar. For specialty drinks such as margaritas or piña coladas, allow 3 1-gallon bottles of tequila, rum, or other liquor per 100 guests. The quantities of mineral water, beer, ice, and sodas may need to be adjusted for warmer weather and climates. For cooler climates, allow for more red wine, and possibly some cognac or brandy. When serving champagne for a toast, figure that you will be able to serve five guests per bottle. When serving cordials, allow 1 bottle per 100 guests. When serving wine at a formal sit-down dinner, allow 2 bottles of white and 1 bottle of red wine per table (10 to 12 people). If you are serving only wine, beer, and soft drinks, increase the wine by at least 25 percent. Remember that it's always best to have a little left over than to run out mid-party.

BEVERAGE SERVICE CHART—BAR SETUP

Number of Guests

	10	25	50	100
Vodka	1 (750 milliliters)	1 (750 milliliters)	2 (1 gallon)	4 (1 gallon)
Scotch	1 (750 milliliters)	1 (750 milliliters)	2 (1 liter)	3 (1 liter)
Gin	1 (750 milliliters)	1 (750 milliliters)	1 (1 liter)	2 (1 liter)
Bourbon	1 (750 milliliters)	1 (750 milliliters)	1 (1 liter)	1 (1 liter)
Canadian	1 (750 milliliters)	1 (750 milliliters)	1 (1 liter)	1 (1 liter)
Rum	1 (750 milliliters)	1 (750 milliliters)	1 (1 liter)	1 (1 liter)
Tequila	1 (750 milliliters)	1 (750 milliliters)	1 (1 liter)	1 (1 liter)
White wine	4 (750 milliliters)	10 (750 milliliters)	18 (750 milliliters)	30 (750 milliliters)
Red wine	1 (750 milliliters)	2 (750 milliliters)	3 (750 milliliters)	5 (750 milliliters)
Regular beer	½ case (12-oz. bottles)	1 case	2 cases	3 cases
Light beer	1 6-pack (12-oz. bottles)	1 case	1 case	1½ cases
Mineral water	3 (1 liter)	6 (1 liter)	12 (1 liter)	18 (1 liter)
Club soda	2 (1 liter)	3 (1 liter)	5 (1 liter)	10 (1 liter)
Tonic water	2 (1 liter)	3 (1 liter)	5 (1 liter)	10 (1 liter)
Cola	2 (1 liter)	3 (1 liter)	5 (1 liter)	10 (1 liter)
Diet cola	2 (1 liter)	3 (1 liter)	5 (1 liter)	10 (1 liter)
7-Up	2 (1 liter)	3 (1 liter)	5 (1 liter)	10 (1 liter)
Orange juice	2 (1 quart)	3 (1 quart)	4 (1 quart)	8 (1 quart)
Grapefruit juice	1 (1 quart)	1 (1 quart)	2 (1 quart)	4 (1 quart)
Cranberry juice	1 (1 quart)	1 (1 quart)	2 (1 quart)	2 (1 quart)
Bloody Mary mix	1 (1 quart)	1 (1 quart)	2 (1 quart)	2 (1 quart)
Dry vermouth	1 (750 milliliters)	1 (750 milliliters)	1 (750 milliliters)	1 (750 milliliters)
Sweet vermouth	1 (750 milliliters)	1 (750 milliliters)	1 (750 milliliters)	1 (750 milliliters)

Fruit Garnishes

	10	25	50	100
Lemons	1	1	2	3
Limes	2	3	6	9
Olives	1 (3-ounce jar)	1 (3-ounce jar)	1 (3-ounce jar)	1 (3-ounce jar)
Cherries	1 (3-ounce jar)	1 (3-ounce jar)	1 (3-ounce jar)	1 (3-ounce jar)
Ice	15 pounds	30 pounds	75 pounds	150 pounds

CHAPTER FIVE

Setting the Table

Dressing Your Table

Setting the table for a party can be one of the most enjoyable aspects of entertaining, because the possibilities for creative expression are endless. (It's also something that can be planned well in advance.) You can go fun and casual, elegantly formal, or anywhere between the two. The table—and its surroundings—should reflect your personality and your aesthetic sense in the same way that what you select to wear to your party does.

After you have decided whether the party you are giving is a formal sit-down dinner, a more casual buffet, or even a picnic, you'll need to establish how you want the table to look. Pick out

There are so many different and intricate ways to fold napkins that it can make your head spin. But there are also some simple yet eye-catching methods, and napkin folding can be done well before the party begins.

your favorite glassware, flatware, china, napkins, tablecloth or place mats, candles, and centerpieces. Arrange the items in a variety of places and combinations until you hit on a look you like. Remember, though, that too many things on the table can be confusing, so don't clutter it up with extraneous stuff.

Color and Pattern

Color plays an important role in the way a table and its accessories and surroundings look; it can provide a simple yet exciting way to decorate your table. Before planning your table, sit at it and take a good look at the room. Definition and contrast will keep the room from looking monochromatic and unexciting. If the room is all white with pastel accents, pick up those accents and work them in as a part of your color theme, or go all white.

Tablecloths are a fun and easy way to pick up accents or play up contrasts. Combine patterns, colors, and fabrics by mixing and matching, using contrasting under- and overcloths (perhaps with the undercloth a solid and the overcloth patterned, or vice versa), and coordinate your napkins accordingly.

Setting a Buffet Table

A key to a successful buffet is to make sure that guests will not have to perform a balancing act by carrying too many things. If guests will sit at a dining table after going through the buffet, set the table with napkins, flatware, and glasses, so that all guests have to carry is their plate. If the seating is more casual, with guests perching or standing wherever, roll up the silverware in napkins and put these at the end of the buffet table, so that guests pick up a napkin and silverware after they've filled their plates.

After you have decided what to serve at your buffet, and well before the day of the party, inventory your serving pieces—platters, bowls, baskets, centerpieces, and other accessories. Place

If many of your guests don't know each other, and at large events such as weddings, place cards are in order. They allow you to mix and match people so that all the chatty, outgoing folks aren't seated together, while all the shy people languish uncomfortably. Two-sided oversized place cards are a clever idea: the people sitting across the table can read the name, too. Even when most of the guests know each other, place cards are still a nice touch, though they're not as necessary.

There are different philosophies about who to seat with whom, but instead of following any set policy, experiment and have fun. For years, common wisdom had it that you didn't seat couples together—but why not? Sometimes it works wonderfully, especially if you know that one half of a couple feels uncomfortable without his or her partner, or you have a couple who don't know anyone else at the party. And it's all right and can be fun to have tables of women only and men only. You may, as the host, also want to leave a seat open at each table so that you can move among the tables between courses. When it comes to seating arrangements, nothing is written in stone.

Themed parties are always a challenge—but can be lots of fun. *From upper left:* For a lingerie shower centerpiece, I purchased bust forms from a display company and added some ivy vines and pale antheriums to soften the form. The cloths and napkins were pastel. Patti Capelli makes extraordinary topiaries: old silver creamers and sugar bowls become home to her one-of-a-kind creations. French wired ribbon weaves a holiday flourish. A collection of banister finials and small vases holding orchids becomes the centerpiece for this dining-room table. The light refracting through the glass adds to the formality of this simple arrangement. On my excursions to local farmer's markets, I sometimes find vegetables I've never seen in the supermarket. These gorgeous purple and white eggplants, in a red cabbage-leaf ceramic bowl, became the centerpiece at a dinner party; the next day they became part of a ratatouille.

Clockwise from top left: A wire cornucopia is filled with flowers, fruits, and vegetables. Complex arrangements like this one cause interesting comments; because there's so much going on here, we kept the linens, china, and candles white. Vibrant-hued dahlias, delphiniums, and alliums are all you need for a casual summer party. Masses of one flower make a bold statement. Even baby's breath, usually used as a filler for arrangements, makes an impact in large quantities. I think hybrid dahlias look best on their own, without other flowers. To keep some interest in the arrangement, I mix them in hot colors for an outstanding centerpiece on a buffet. Two-sided place cards help guests remember who's sitting across from them.

SETTING-THE-TABLE CHECKLIST

✧ *How many tables do you need?*

✧ *Do you need a seating plan?*

✧ *What do you need on the table?*

   (To a great extent, this will depend on the menu.)

      service plates

      salad plates

      bread-and-butter plates

      dinner plates

      flatware

      glasses

✧ *Take an inventory of your china, glassware, and flatware.*

✧ *Determine a color scheme.*

✧ *Plan what you want to use for centerpieces and*
   where you want to put them.

✧ *Set a "trial table" to make sure you have enough of everything.*
   Sit down at the table. Is it comfortably appointed, or is it
   too cluttered?

✧ *Determine whether you will serve family-style or with plates*
   that have been arranged in the kitchen, or whether guests
   will serve themselves from a buffet.

✧ *Select linens, napkin rings, and candlesticks.*

them on the buffet until the arrangement looks the way you want it. Label each serving piece as to where it will be placed and what it will hold (be sure to remove the labels before you serve!).

As a rule, food looks more sumptuous on platters and in shallow containers than in deep bowls or baskets. It's also easier for guests to choose their portion when they're not digging into a bowl.

Make sure that your buffet table is easily accessible to your guests. You want there to be enough room so that there isn't a mad crunch to get to it and so that, once there, the lines aren't too long. If you have the space, place your buffet table in the center of the room so traffic can flow on both sides. Often, however, the only option is a sideboard or a table against a wall. To make this arrangement more workable, avoid foods that require carving, assembly, or anything else that would cause delays. Have one table of guests go to the buffet at a time (if it's a party with more than one table), or do "doubles," setting the buffet with two of each dish, starting at the ends and working toward the middle.

Centerpieces

A centerpiece can add so much to how a table and the room in general look, from dramatic flair to romantic softness.

While flowers are the most popular, and do make beautiful centerpieces, they are best when simply arranged, perhaps using one type, such as fresh-cut garden roses, or a mixed bouquet unified by color—a vase of pale white tulips, roses, and peonies can look sensational. Or group a few vases together or place them on different areas of the table, filling each vase with a varied yet similarly themed arrangement.

One caveat with flowers: take care to choose flowers with mild fragrances when the food you're serving is highly spiced or aromatic; you don't want the odors to compete.

Fruits and vegetables also make enchanting centerpieces. What could be more beautiful than a basket overflowing with pears, or a cobalt glass bowl filled with lemons wreathed with lemon leaves, or a wooden board massed with pyramids of rich red pomegranates? Ripe fruits will scent the room as deliciously as flowers, and fruits and vegetables won't wilt in hot weather, as flowers may. Take terrific-looking baskets and fill them with different kinds and colors of squash and peppers, or go with a monochrome theme. These centerpieces are recyclable in the best way—just cook them up the next day.

Using objects as centerpieces can be very effective, too. A small sculpture, a piece of pottery, or candlesticks of varying heights, grouped together in a combination of shapes and styles, can look quite striking on a table. Small potted plants, especially in groupings, look great.

Centerpieces are a terrific way to emphasize the theme of the party. At a breakfast or brunch party, use wire chicken-shaped baskets filled with fresh brown eggs. For the holidays, heap baskets full of rosy red apples, or bowls of pine cones sprayed gold. At a baby shower, how about using soft cloth diapers as napkins, vases of baby's breath, and glass baby bottles with a straw for serving beverages in?

No matter what type of centerpiece you choose, one rule of thumb is to make sure that your guests can see across the table to each other. Small topiary and flower arrangements should be no taller than 12 inches high, and the stems of tall topi-

Right: from top to bottom:
It's amazing to watch a rented blank plywood round table transformed into a beautiful setting. Place a black round cloth on the table. You want it long enough so that the metal legs are out of sight. Place an ivory round cloth, the same size as the black cloth, on top of the black cloth. Gather it in four spots and tie with French wired ribbon. Brass chargers, napkins tied with more wired ribbon, faceted glassware, some gold columns from my collection, and beeswax candles complete the transformation.

The variety of attractive paper goods is astounding. Many companies have coordinated tablecloths and napkins, along with cups and flatware. Pick elements from the invitation—specifically the grape cluster and ivy—and use them as the centerpiece to pull this look together.

Take out the linens that you've been saving for a special occasion—that occasion is now. Use the things you love.

Left: from top to bottom:
To fan-fold a napkin, first fold the napkin in half.
Next, accordian-fold the napkin in 1 ½-inch pleats lengthwise, using a little pressure to make the creases.
Now, fold the pleated napkin in half.
To finish, pinch the folded napkin two-thirds up from the bottom and place either on the service plate, or between the silverware if you're not using a service plate.

aries should be at least 20 inches high. Guests should not feel as though they need machetes to hack through foliage to talk.

Centerpieces for the serving table at a buffet, however, can be grander and more bold than those on dining tables. Sometimes placing the centerpiece off to one side rather than in the center of a table can add a note of drama. Here are some ideas for buffet centerpieces:

✧ *Garnish cake stands with candied fruits or votive candles.*

✧ *Arrange taller flowers in favorite vases.*

✧ *Mass pots of orchids, baby roses, herbs, or other blooming plants.*

✧ *Group objects, such as sculptures or candlesticks.*

Rentals

Rental companies are an invaluable source for larger parties, and can supply just about anything you will need. A full-service rental company can provide not only table settings but also tenting, lighting, sound systems, kitchen grills, barbecues, all manner of chairs and tables, linens, bars, cooking equipment, coffeemakers, and even trash cans, chilling tubs, coat racks, stanchions and chains, folding screens, and podiums.

While the cost of renting equipment can add up, it's often worth the expense if you do not have enough of everything or are worried about breakage.

A rental company will generally send a representative to your home or the party location (you can visit the showroom as well) and show you samples of what it has to offer. Some rental agencies can offer assistance with planning the space and can put you in touch with other party professionals, should you need them.

Paper Goods

While paper and plastic serving pieces may not be appropriate for every party, disposable party goods have improved tremendously over the past few years. There are so many beautiful paper and plastic dishware lines available now, with coordinating tablecloths, napkins, flatware, glassware, centerpieces, and other accessories, that sometimes it is difficult to tell them from their breakable counterparts.

Disposables are best saved for large parties, outdoor parties, barbecues, picnics, informal buffets, and, of course, children's parties.

CHAPTER SIX

Lights, Camera, Music, Action!

I f you've ever seen a stage production, you know how important lighting and music are in creating a mood. Think of your party as your own personal theatrical production. A wise director is aware that no single element of a production should call too much attention to itself; all the components should blend, working together to form a whole. While the lighting and music should be subtle enough to remain in the background (unless your event is based around music or dancing), these are two details that have the power to shape your party.

Opposite: Candlelight is the most romantic and flattering. Gather all your candlesticks from tables and niches, and your pyramid cake stands, and then load everything with candles and votives.

Counterclockwise from upper left: Glass votive inserts in this sculptured iron piece solve a lighting and centerpiece problem simultaneously. The fiorelli pears and lady apples could be substituted with other fruits, flowers, or vegetables.

Fill an unglazed terra-cotta pot or a favorite bowl or container with sand, and then arrange the candles in spoke fashion. Allow for some dripping here. When the candles are exposed, as they are here, position them away from draperies or your guests' sleeves, and out of the reach of children.

Candles have to be shielded from the breeze when used outdoors. Hurricanes are readily available at hardware stores, specialty houseware shops, and sometimes through rental companies. A terra-cotta pot is covered with moss, and Styrofoam is inserted into the pot. Finish with a candle, some more votives, and *voilà!* light and a great-looking arrangement.

Indoor Lighting

Creating your lighting plan should be done well before the party, and light is a terrifically fun element to play with. If you don't already have dimmer switches, installing them is easy and affordable. Experiment with different types of lightbulbs, perhaps trying soft pink or candle-light-look bulbs in floor or table lamps. If you have overhead or track lighting, adjust the angles of the beams by moving the cans or using paper shades. Have a dress rehearsal with your lights to see how changing the wattage or the focus affects the look of the room.

The level of light is especially important. Too bright, and your guests may feel it's "closing time"—few things can clear a room more quickly than turning the lights up all the way. On the other hand, you don't want your guests plunged into murky darkness, wishing they had brought pocket flashlights. Guests should have no problem in discerning the food they are eating or the people they're conversing with.

Once you've selected a level of light that's comfortable, be sure that it is consistent throughout the entire party space. The intensity should not vary from room to room.

Lighting also plays an important role in relation to the food you are serving. Food that is directly spotlit becomes the center of attention. Table settings, and, with buffets, the tables themselves, must be arranged so that they are lighted in a flattering way. Fluorescent lights can sometimes appear to change the colors of foods, so you may want to switch to color-corrected or warm-toned fluorescent bulbs, if they are available.

You can also illuminate plants or favorite objects dramatically with the use of strategically placed spotlights. Add a festive twinkle to indoor trees or larger plants by stringing them with lights—another inexpensive yet beautiful way to give any event a special-occasion touch.

One of the most effective and glamorous ways to light a party is candlelight. It is incredibly romantic, softly flattering to everyone, and can even become a theme in itself. Tables adorned with collections of candlesticks and candelabra, flickering with tiny golden flames, are a breathtaking sight. Cull candlesticks from their usual niches and mass them together on mantels, tables, sideboards—just about anywhere. Mix candles of different heights, widths, and colors in all manner of holders. If you run short of candlesticks, tie bunches of candles together with florists' twine or ribbon and set them on an interesting plate or in a shallow bowl.

Votive candles look wonderful scattered the length of a table or at each place setting. Hurricane lamps are another way of using candlelight; the glass sheath not only protects the candle inside, but also seems to refract and magnify the light. And if you want to spotlight a favorite object, placing a candle next to it will do the trick.

When using candles, light them before your guests arrive so that their lovely glow is already in effect.

Outdoor Lighting

Like indoor lighting, outdoor lighting is best planned in advance. Take a good look at the space during the same span of time that the party is to take place. If the party will end after sunset, you must light accordingly. If your house has backyard lighting, make sure that the floodlights are properly positioned—again, do a dress rehearsal with the lights.

Using candles outdoors can look quite beautiful and dramatic, but do remember to shield them against breezes. Hurricane lamps and votive and other glass containers are best. Another pretty, creative idea is to use *luminarios*, traditional Mexican candleholders: decorate paper bags with cutouts, place a scoop of sand in the bottom, and set a votive candle in a glass holder in the sand. These look wonderful lining a pathway, on tabletops, or around a pool. Be sure to use glass holders so the bag won't ignite.

Citronella candles are another nice touch. Sold in houseware, hardware, garden, and party stores, these seem to keep bugs, bees, and other flying fauna away, and are often attractively packaged in little galvanized metal pails or terra-cotta pots. They also come on stakes that can be used like tiki lamps—just stick them in the ground wherever you want the light.

Candlelight at an outdoor event can be really effective, festive, and beautiful. Remember your light levels. If you are combining electric light with candlelight, make sure that the electric light is kept dim enough to allow the candles to glow.

Always be aware of the hazardous side of candlelight: don't place candles on precarious ledges where they may fall or be knocked over, or in places where people may have to reach over them risking a fiery sleeve. Keep candles away from dried flowers or any other flammable objects. Be aware of wax dripping: make sure that the melted wax won't land where you don't want it to. And the only place for them at a children's party is on the birthday cake!

Above: Lighting levels that vary from room to room are disconcerting; it takes time for your eyes to adjust. A dress rehearsal for the lights at your party well in advance will allow you the time to install dimmers and fine-tune the light.

Left: Overhead recessed spotlights add drama. By dimming the other lights in the room, the flowers and the food become the center of attention.

Counterclockwise from top left:
Luminarios act as both a lighting element and a path to the entrance to this party. Fill the paper bags with sand and place the votive candle in glass holders to prevent the bags from igniting. I love this basket for a casual outdoor centerpiece, though the wind will eventually blow the candles out. When pomegranates aren't in season, I use fruits or vegetables that are. Position in the light what you want to stand out. This arrangement, placed under a spotlight, is breathtaking.

Music and Entertainment

Music and other types of entertainment are festive ways to enliven and enhance your party. Because one of the purposes of a party is to give people a chance to meet and chat with one another, music especially should ideally provide a pleasant background. Like lighting, these elements are just ingredients to be blended into the whole. Unless at some point you are featuring a performer, the entertainment at your party should not call undue attention to itself. It's a different story if your party is based around a recital, dance, or other performance; otherwise, the entertainment should not overwhelm the festivities and become the focus of the event. Think of it as an accessory, or a side dish, as it were—not a main course.

The music that you select for your party should fit the occasion. For a small, at-home dinner party, recorded music playing softly in the background will do just fine. (Avoid radio music, as commercials and station breaks prove distracting.) One option is to record tapes with a selection of songs or instrumental pieces you particularly like. A number of record stores offer a service called Personics, which catalogs thousands of songs that can be recorded onto a cassette while you wait. Programmable compact-disc carousels are another great way to get hours of uninterrupted music.

For larger parties, music can be more pronounced. While this doesn't mean you need to hire a five-piece band, if it is within your budget, live music is preferable. Consider hiring a music student or pianist to play your piano; for a Christmas party, have some carolers entertain; a Mexican fiesta might call for mariachis; an afternoon tea, for a harpist.

To find musicians, ask among your friends, check with the music departments of local colleges or music schools, churches, synagogues, or even a small talent agency. If it isn't in your budget to hire musicians, every kind of music imaginable is available on records, tapes, and CDs. In addition, many libraries have extensive recorded-music collections for you to check out.

Other Entertainment

For certain types of parties—anniversaries, graduations, bar or bat mitzvahs, and children's birthdays—you may wish to bring in other entertainers. Celebrity impersonators, cabaret performers, fortunetellers, clowns, caricature artists, and dancers, for starters, can be novel, and an appearance by Santa Claus can just about make a Christmas party.

If you see an act that you enjoy at someone else's party, be sure to get the act's card and ask that host for a reference. Otherwise, to find exactly what you are looking for, check with party planners, the performing-arts department of a local college or university, or talent agencies. Don't hire *anyone*, even on a recommendation, sight unseen. Ask to see a performance or a videotape of one well before your event is to take place. If your party has a specific theme, or you would like the musicians to dress in a certain mode, be sure to specify that.

Say "Cheese"

If you want to have your event photographed or videotaped, follow the same guidelines as for hiring entertainment. Ask to see a portfolio or samples of videos before hiring anyone. Make sure that the photographer or video-camera operator won't be too intrusive; few guests like to have bright lights, flashing strobes, or microphones shoved into their faces at a party.

HOST ETIQUETTE

As a host, you have a set of obligations toward your guests. Most of these are very simple, yet meeting them will go a long way toward ensuring that your party will be all you want it to be. The following are some guidelines.

✧ *Your invitation should clearly state all the pertinent information: date, time, place, mode of dress, indoors or out, and the type of party it will be.*

✧ *Be conscious of putting together a good guest mix. Think of your guests as a palette; you don't want a monochromatic party. You may be surprised by who hits it off with whom.*

✧ *Bathrooms should be well stocked with fresh soap, guest towels, and plenty of toilet paper— and make sure that the doors lock.*

✧ *Be sure to introduce people. Some guests are shy and uncomfortable introducing themselves*

to people they do not know; it is up to you, as the host, to touch base with everyone and make sure that everyone knows who everyone else is. While this isn't always possible at large events, keep your eyes open for any guests who look adrift, and get them involved. Always try to put your guests at ease.

✧ *When serving food, have something for those who are vegetarian or on restricted diets. Simply providing a healthful selection of side dishes should suffice. If some guests are on a diet plan and insist on bringing their own food, let them.*

✧ *If a guest has too much to drink, offer to call a taxi or have another guest drive him or her home. You may have to become insistent, but better to be a bit of a scold than take any chances. If a guest gets disruptive or abusive, you may have to ask him or her to leave.*

✧ *For guests who want to smoke in a nonsmoking house, short of posting a No Smoking sign, you will have to tell guests that they may smoke outside. An absence of ashtrays may help to deter some people, but die-hard smokers will use any available plate or glass for their ashes.*

✧ *Any belongings that you are particularly concerned about, such as prescription medications or jewelry, should be safely stored.*

✧ *If a guest asks if he or she can bring a couple of friends along to your party, that is your call. If you are not comfortable with this, or if it's too much of an imposition, say no. You don't have to give a reason why.*

If your guests will be sitting for a long time, they'll need protection. Huge market umbrellas serve as a shield from intense sun, but don't obscure the breathtaking ocean view.

Put the finishing touches on the table before the guests arrive, but don't light the candles until just before the guests are seated.

Larger parties need more help than smaller ones. Depending on the size of your budget, staffing agencies that specialize in parties are invaluable, but students and housekeepers can lend a hand.

The colors of the tablecloths on the bar pick up the colors of the foliage and the ocean, and contrast with the terra-cotta tiled patio. The bartenders are dressed casually in all white. Have the staff dress according to your event; though common, black bow ties and tux shirts are not always appropriate.

While, for the most part, thank-you notes seem to have gone the way of the horse and buggy, they are a thoughtful gesture—a tradition that serves an important purpose, for both host and guest. As the host, you needn't, of course, send every one of your guests a thank-you simply for attending; however, if a gift is brought, even if it is flowers or a little bread-and-butter trinket for a dinner party, a thank-you note should be sent. It's a simple acknowledgment that really means a lot.

Guest Etiquette

There is a code of behavior for guests just as there is for hosts. Here are a few simple yet vital guidelines for attending a party.

✧ *Arrive on time. Unless you are the guest of honor, remember that the party does not revolve around you.*

✧ *Respond to the invitation, and do so in a timely manner. Just showing up can throw off the balance of a party as far as the food service and seating arrangements are concerned.*

✧ *Even if the party does not warrant a gift, a little trinket, some exquisite candies, a potted plant, a bottle of wine, champagne, or a cordial, or a box of lovely soaps brought to the host is a very thoughtful gesture.*

✧ *Don't bring cut flowers as a gift; they may not go with the decor of the party, and it also means that the host has to fuss with arranging them.*

However, flowers sent the next day as a thank-you are a wonderful gesture.

✧ *Don't bring food for the party (unless it is a potluck, of course).*

✧ *If you smoke, be sure to ask what the smoking policy in the host's home is before lighting up.*

✧ *Don't arrive with an entourage of uninvited guests.*

✧ *Leave your cellular phone or beeper in the car unless you are a doctor or are expecting some important news.*

✧ *Don't bring children or pets unless they are specifically invited or you have already cleared this with your host.*

✧ *A little thank-you note shows a great deal of thoughtfulness. It is something that takes but a couple of minutes, yet so few of us take the time to do it—it really makes a host feel that the party was truly enjoyed by the guests who were a part of it.*

Troubleshooting

Whether you are having four guests or forty, even the most seasoned host experiences that knot-in-the-stomach feeling of anticipation. Even when the menu is simple and you are eating in the kitchen, you tend to worry, "Is everything going to be all right?"

Some anxiety is a part of entertaining. But keep things in perspective; you do want to enjoy yourself at your own event. After all, it is a party, not an invasion; your world won't end if it isn't a smashing success.

If some disaster should happen, it's less catastrophic if you have a contingency plan—an indoor alternative to the lakeside park if the day of your party is rainy.

Being prepared also means having everything that can possibly be done in advance done. Some last-minute details, such as finishing touches on certain foods or setting out the ice buckets, are unavoidable. But the more you can do prior to the party, the less you will worry, and the greater your enjoyment will be.

Sometimes, when a party has been weeks or even months in the planning, it may seem as though you have had the party experience well before the actual event takes place. So don't overdo your preplanning—that can be just as deleterious as underplanning. You want to have fun, too.

CHAPTER SEVEN

Special Parties

WEDDINGS

First things first: no matter how tense and frenzied things may get, everyone planning a wedding should keep foremost in his or her mind the phrase "Weddings are happy occasions, weddings are happy occasions." This little thought often gets forgotten in the common, yet not always necessary, roil of wedding plans.

Weddings are so completely different from any other type of party that they really are a genre unto themselves. They are very emotional, and because there is more than one person getting married, more than one family involved in making choices and decisions, planning a wedding can become fraught with tension and stress. There is a bride to please, a groom to please, two sets of parents, and then some.

It is the most important day in many people's lives, yet because the road leading up to it is often littered with hurt and bad feelings, it isn't always the happiest. No matter how simple and streamlined you may try to keep your wedding, things always seem to get complicated. Everything seems to be at fever pitch.

While it is impossible to promise that if you follow a well-mapped-out plan your wedding reception will go without a hitch, planning certainly can help eliminate a lot of problems.

Depending on the level of formality and how involved future in-laws are, it is best, once the couple is engaged and has chosen a time frame for the wedding, for all the interested parties to meet and get everything out on the table. Decisions should be made as to the size of the wedding, the budget, and who is to be responsible financially for what. Even couples who are planning and paying for their wedding themselves will find that they are being given advice and suggestions by parents. If everyone's role is clearly defined, tension and confusion can be avoided.

If you opt for a wedding at home, the size of your guest list should be consistent with the number of people who can fit comfortably in your house. While it is certainly possible to act as caterer for your own wedding, remember that you are going to be very preoccupied with other matters. Think about this carefully; you may be better off hiring a caterer than doing it yourself. If you want to do the cooking yourself, don't get in over your head by preparing food for one hundred people when the most you've ever cooked for is six. Unless you're a VERY proficient baker, it's best to

buy a cake. Enlist the help of friends and relatives, and hire someone to assist you in the preparations before the wedding, as well as for the wedding day.

Planning the Big Day

A wedding celebration involves a whole different set of details. There are a wealth of books and guides that will advise you on the ins and outs of putting on a wedding, wedding protocol, and etiquette. You can take information from any or all of them and tailor them to your needs, or you may want to call in the services of a wedding planner, who can help you plan your entire event. The planner can also put you in touch with caterers, florists, rental companies, musicians, photographers, videotapers, printers, bakers, and so forth.

You can pick virtually any time of the day to do a wedding; just plan the food to go along with that time frame. Make it clear on your invitation whether the wedding will be "reception only," "reception following the ceremony," "dinner following . . . ," "brunch following . . . ," and so on.

STRICTLY BUSINESS

What makes a business party different from any other party? It's your boss and colleagues who are coming to your home, and that can be a little nerve-racking. Whatever image you project — whether ultrachic and sophisticated or more subtle and casual — it shouldn't be too far from your office persona. The tenor of the party depends on your objective—what you would like to achieve with this party.

Inviting someone into your home is an intimate gesture. At work, you are on common ground, but when your co-workers are on your turf, you can use that to your advantage. The most important thing to remember about business entertaining is to do it in a way you are perfectly comfortable with. This isn't the time for surprises and experiments.

If you have children, have them fed and in bed before your guests arrive. If you are not inviting all of the people in your office or department, particularly if it is a fairly small one, don't talk about the event in front of the noninvitees before, or after. That only leads to hurt feelings and resentments, and you have to see these people every day.

FOR CHILDREN ONLY

The key to throwing a successful children's party is to remember these parties are more about visuals and entertainment—food is secondary (although still important).

You can really have a great time decorating your child's party. Make the space wonderful by using balloons (renting a helium tank from a party specialty shop or balloon store and doing it yourself is easy), whimsical favors, hand puppets, inexpensive wind-up toys—let your (and your kid's) imagination run wild. Just make sure that the decorations and favors are age-appropriate, with no small parts or sharp edges.

Keep the food simple, and serve kids' favorite things. Pizza, sandwiches, burgers, hot dogs, popcorn, unsalted or low-salt chips, and delicious homemade or bakery cookies are easy, fun alternatives to junk food.

Be sure to have lots of age-appropriate activities planned; we all know how short kids' attention spans are. In addition to popular games or holiday activities like Easter egg hunts, celebrity impersonators, whether a cartoon character or a teen superstar, can be a kick. Something kids can make (under adult supervision), such as tie-dyed or hand-painted T-shirts, collages, or another craft, provides a great time at the party and gives each guest a unique souvenir to take home.

If you opt to have your child's party somewhere other than your home, there are a wealth of locations at your disposal. Parties at children's gyms are a good idea, as gyms generally have staff who will supervise and plan games for the children; you just need to provide the food, accessories, and decorations. You can also go on an excursion to a park, historical site, circus, or children's play, and make it an exciting adventure, packing a box lunch for each child.

Choose a theme based on your child's most passionate interest—dinosaurs or baseball or a favorite movie or television character. And kids' parties are the one type of party at which you should definitely use disposable goods. Most party, card, and specialty stores carry extensive lines of paper and plastic goods featuring various characters and themes, complete with plates, "silverware," centerpieces, tablecloths, napkins, invitations, and party favors that all coordinate.

Counterclockwise from top left:
Before the wedding ceremony, the flower girls and the ring bearer check out the party scene.
Black-tie weddings call for formal attire for band members. It's best not to assume that the band will be dressed appropriately; communicate your specifics well before your party. The bride and the groom are usually the last to sit down at their wedding, and are often too nervous to eat much. I always pack a beautiful basket for the morning after, full of tastes from the night before. Remember to budget for additional lighting if your wedding is at night and outdoors.

Counterclockwise from top left:
Kids' parties are perfect for great-looking disposable paper and plastic products. Food is secondary—playing with these cutout sandwiches is more fun than eating them.
Make sure that toys and favors are age-appropriate; these animal noses are safe for children over age three, and kids think they're hysterical.
Simple foods—sandwiches on whole wheat bread and fresh fruit—are best for kids' parties.
Felt hand puppet centerpieces complete the farm theme and will be given to the children as favors.

PART TWO

Party Menus

How to Use the Recipes in This Section

These suggested menus and recipes are very eclectic in their combination of ingredients and dishes. Each recipe—in fact, each menu—has been used for actual parties; they are tried and true.

Please note that oven temperatures vary, and that altitude affects cooking times as well, so take this into consideration when you prepare these recipes. Most of the ingredients used in these recipes are generally available. We have noted where harder-to-find ingredients may be found, or where substitutions can be made.

The Breakfast Party

Time to Serve: Before 11:00 A.M.

The idea of giving a breakfast party may seem a little bit unusual, but if you and your guests are morning people, entertaining early in the day can be a great way to get friends together for a leisurely weekend meal, or an effective tool for running a business meeting. Your menu can be as simple as freshly squeezed fruit juice, aromatic coffee and tea, delicious muffins or coffee cake, and interesting cereals or homemade granolas—or have your guests tuck into heartier fare, like pancakes, waffles, French toast, omelettes, or breakfast sandwiches.

When hosting a breakfast party, you don't want to be stuck at the stove, making dishes to order for each guest. Plan a menu that will avoid a lot of last-minute preparation so you're free to enjoy your guests. Whether you bring everything to the table family-style or serve your guests individually, your breakfast menu should not depend on carefully orchestrating everything being done at the same time.

This breakfast menu is a hearty one. Freshly squeezed orange or grapefruit juice, or perhaps a more exotic blend, like strawberry-papaya, will perfectly complement it. A cup of freshly ground coffee (it's best to offer both regular and decaf) and some full-bodied teas provide the final fillip that makes for a great breakfast.

French Toast Stuffed with Peanut Butter and Bananas

Homemade Chicken-and-Apple Sausage Patties

Freshly Squeezed Juice

Coffee and Tea

French Toast Stuffed with Peanut Butter and Bananas and Homemade Chicken-and-Apple Sausage Patties

French Toast Stuffed with Peanut Butter and Bananas

Serves 6

This sounds like a heavy dish, but it actually isn't; children and adults love peanut butter.

7 ripe bananas
2 tablespoons (¼ stick) unsalted butter
3 tablespoons granulated sugar
1 or 2 loaves egg bread (such as challah), cut into nine 1½-inch-thick slices
1 cup plus 2 tablespoons creamy peanut butter

6 ripe bananas

2 tablespoons (¼ stick) unsalted butter
2 tablespoons granulated sugar

6 large eggs
2 tablespoons granulated sugar
2½ cups milk
10 tablespoons (1¼ sticks) unsalted butter
Confectioners' sugar
Maple syrup

First, prepare the bananas for the stuffing: Peel the 7 bananas and cut each on an angle into 10 to 12 pieces. In a medium nonstick skillet set over medium heat, melt the 2 tablespoons of butter. Add the banana pieces to the skillet and sprinkle with the 3 tablespoons of sugar. Sauté, stirring gently, for 6 to 7 minutes, or until the bananas are soft but not mushy. Remove from the heat and set aside.

Cut each slice of bread in half on the diagonal. Make a pocket in each triangle by slicing the top not completely through, leaving ½ inch uncut. Open the pocket and spread 1 teaspoon of peanut butter on each side. Put 3 to 4 slices of sautéed banana on one side. Close the pocket by pushing the two sides together. (The French toast can be made up to this point the day before and refrigerated.)

Next, prepare the bananas for caramelizing: Peel the 6 bananas and cut each on an angle into 9 pieces. In a medium nonstick skillet set over medium-high heat, melt the 2 tablespoons of butter. Add the banana pieces to the skillet and sprinkle with the 2 tablespoons of sugar. Cook on each side for 3 to 5 minutes, or until the bananas are browned and crisp. Remove from the heat and set aside.

Now, prepare the French toast: In a large bowl, beat the 6 eggs and the 2 tablespoons of sugar with a fork until just blended. Add the 2½ cups of milk and beat a few more strokes.

In a large nonstick skillet set over medium heat, melt 2 tablespoons of the butter. Dip each stuffed pocket sandwich into the egg-and-milk mixture and sauté it on each side up to 6 minutes, or until golden brown. Repeat with additional butter until all the pockets are done. Do as many at a time as will fit in the skillet without touching.

If you are not serving immediately, set these aside. When ready to serve, preheat the oven to 300° F, place the French toast on a cookie sheet, and heat for 15 minutes, until warmed through.

To serve, decorate each piece of French toast with 3 slices of caramelized banana, and dust with confectioners' sugar. Serve with maple syrup.

Homemade Chicken-and-Apple Sausage Patties

Serves 6

These scrumptious sausages are not necessarily just for breakfast: they could be served at other times of the day.

3 ounces dried apples
¼ cup hot water
1 pound ground chicken
1 egg white
½ cup applesauce
1 teaspoon ground fennel
¼ teaspoon curry powder
1 tablespoon grated onion
1 tablespoon grated fresh ginger
½ teaspoon ground coriander
¼ teaspoon white pepper
1½ teaspoons salt
¼ cup flour
Vegetable oil

Soak the dried apples in the hot water for 10 to 15 minutes, or until soft. Drain and chop them medium-fine.

In a large bowl, mix the ground chicken with the egg white, applesauce, fennel, curry, grated onion, ginger, coriander, pepper, salt, and flour with a wooden spoon until well combined. Cover the bowl with plastic wrap and refrigerate for at least 15 minutes. Remove from the refrigerator and form the chicken mixture into twelve 3½-inch-round patties.

In a medium skillet set over medium heat, heat just enough oil to coat the bottom of the pan and sauté the patties on one side for about 5 minutes, or until golden. Turn the patties and cook for about 3 minutes more, or until cooked through and golden on the outside. If necessary, add more oil and sauté the remaining patties.

(These can be made the day before and refrigerated. To serve, preheat the oven to 300° F, place the patties on a cookie sheet, and heat for 12 to 15 minutes, until warmed through.)

The Brunch Party

Time to Serve: Between 10:00 A.M. and 2:00 P.M.

Because so many restaurants and hotels offer brunch in every manner of cuisine and style, this meal has become a weekend tradition that seems to involve going out more than serving at home. But don't forget that having brunch at home can be just as special as having it out.

Brunches can be formal and elegant, or very casual, depending on your menu and presentation. Whether it's served indoors or out, on your finest china or funkiest Depression glass, brunch offers a multitude of culinary opportunities. By nature, it is a relaxing, convivial meal, the perfect time to dust off that old coffee or tea service that you stuck up on a high shelf. Brunch is also the perfect buffet meal. Because it encompasses breakfast and lunch fare, you have a lot of latitude as to what you can serve—give your creativity free rein when you plan the menu. Just follow this rule of thumb: If you plan to eat before noon, serve more breakfast dishes; after noon, the menu should lean more toward lunch.

This brunch menu is a well-rounded one; there's meat for the meat eaters and plenty of other choices for those who prefer to avoid it.

Some good beverages for this brunch would be festive blended drinks such as Bloody Marys, mimosas, or Bellinis. You can make "virgin" versions with nonalcoholic champagne for the last two, and by simply leaving the vodka out of the Bloody Marys. Be sure to offer freshly ground coffee and decaf, as well as a selection of herbal, flavored, and international teas.

Brunch Party Menu—Serves 18

Glazed Whole Salami

Baked Frittata with Zucchini, Lemon, and Leeks

Platter of Berries, Melons, and Exotic Fruits

with Poppy-Seed Dressing

Cucumber, Garden Tomato, and Feta Salad

Mocha-Cocoa-Nut Muffins

Apricot-Almond Loaf with Sweetened Goat Cheese

Glazed Whole Salami

Serves 18

This baked and glazed salami is so easy and so tasty. It's a recipe that's been around for years, and for good reason. If you prefer, substitute a whole Canadian bacon for the salami.

1 5-pound kosher salami
1½ cups apricot preserves
¾ cup grainy country-style mustard

Preheat the oven to 350° F.

Score the top of the salami as you would a ham: make ¾-inch-deep crosscuts about ½ inch apart. Put the salami in a large baking pan and place in the oven.

While the salami is cooking, mix the apricot preserves and the mustard. When the salami has baked for 30 minutes, remove it from the oven and cover it with the glaze. Increase the heat to 450° F, return the salami to the oven, and bake for another 20 to 30 minutes, until it looks caramelized. Remove from the oven and cool to room temperature before cutting into ¼-inch slices.

(This can be made the day before and heated in a 300° F oven for 15 to 20 minutes, just enough to warm through. Do not slice the salami until you are ready to serve it.)

Glazed Whole Salami

Baked Frittata with Zucchini, Lemon, and Leeks

Makes three 9-inch frittatas, yielding 18 to 24 wedges

Basically, a frittata is a quiche without a crust and without the cream; because there is no pastry, it tends to be lighter. The lemon zest in this frittata adds a fresh taste.

6 medium zucchini, coarsely shredded (about 3 pounds)
3 teaspoons salt
½ cup extra-virgin olive oil
6 large red potatoes, peeled and sliced ¼ inch thick
1 large bunch leeks, white part only, ⅛ inch thick (about 1 cup)
4 large garlic cloves, minced
18 large eggs
½ pound Provolone cheese, coarsely shredded
¼ cup finely grated Parmesan cheese
1 teaspoon freshly ground black pepper
2 tablespoons finely chopped flat-leaf parsley
4 tablespoons finely chopped fresh basil
1½ tablespoons grated lemon zest

Preheat the oven to 325° F. Coat three 9-inch round cake pans with vegetable-oil cooking spray. Set aside.

In a large bowl, mix the shredded zucchini with 1½ teaspoons of the salt. Transfer the zucchini to a colander and let drain for 30 minutes. Then squeeze out as much of the liquid as possible.

In a large nonstick skillet set over medium-high heat, heat ¼ cup of the olive oil. Sauté the potato slices on both sides until golden, about 10 minutes. Remove the potatoes from the skillet and set aside.

Heat the remaining ¼ cup of olive oil in the same skillet. Reduce the heat to medium, add the sliced leeks, and sauté for 5 minutes, or until the leeks wilt. Add the garlic and cook, stirring, for 10 seconds, or until fragrant. Remove the skillet from the heat and set aside.

Baked Frittata with
Zucchini, Lemon,
and Leeks

Cucumber, Garden
Tomato, and
Feta Salad

Platter of Berries,
Melons, and
Exotic Fruits

Mocha-Cocoa-Nut
Muffins

Apricot-Almond Loaf with
Sweetened Goat Cheese

In a very large bowl, beat the eggs well. Add the zucchini, leeks, Provolone and Parmesan cheeses, the remaining 1½ teaspoons salt, pepper, parsley, basil, and lemon zest; mix well.

Cover the bottoms of the prepared cake pans with the potato slices. Pour the egg mixture over the potatoes, making sure that it is evenly divided among the three pans. Bake for 30 to 45 minutes, or until the eggs have set. If necessary, rotate the pans midway through baking.

Remove from the oven and invert each fritatta by covering the cake pan with a serving plate and flipping the two together. Cut each frittata into 6 to 8 wedges, and serve at once.

(This dish is best when it is served right away, though room temperature is fine. However, the texture changes if you refrigerate it.)

Platter of Berries, Melons, and Exotic Fruits

Serves 18

The freshest fruits make all the difference in this dish. Vary what you use depending on what is in season, or what your favorite fruits are. The zesty Poppy-Seed Dressing is an adaptation of a terrific recipe from *James Beard's American Cooking.*

4 pints strawberries
1½ pounds Bing cherries
1 large pink grapefruit
1 large, ripe, but firm papaya
1 small honeydew melon
½ seedless watermelon
1 pineapple
2 ripe but firm mangoes
Poppy-Seed Dressing (recipe follows)

Rinse the strawberries and the cherries and dry them well. Peel and section the grapefruit. Peel the papaya,

cut it in half, remove the seeds, and cut it into wedges. Remove the rind and seeds from the honeydew, and cut it into wedges. Remove the rind from the watermelon and cut it into triangular slices. Peel and core the pineapple, cut it in half lengthwise, then cut each half into ¼-inch slices.

To prepare the mangoes, cut off both sides of the mango lengthwise, discarding the fibrous pit. Score each half crosswise, ½ inch apart, leaving the skin intact. Invert the mango by pressing the skin with your fingertips.

Arrange the fruits on a large platter, and serve with Poppy-Seed Dressing on the side.

(The fruit can be cleaned and prepared the night before, but make sure to dry it thoroughly and cover with a paper or cloth towel. Don't combine the fruits until ready to serve. The platter can be assembled up to one hour before serving.)

Poppy-Seed Dressing

Makes about 2 cups

1½ teaspoons dry mustard
1½ teaspoons salt
1⅓ cups sugar
2 tablespoons grated red onion
2 tablespoons fresh lemon juice
¼ cup red-wine vinegar
1½ cups vegetable oil
2½ tablespoons poppy seeds

In the bowl of a food processor fitted with the metal blade, combine the mustard, salt, sugar, onion, lemon juice, and vinegar. Process for a few seconds, until the ingredients are well mixed. With the motor running, add the oil in a thin, steady stream, until it is incorporated and the mixture begins to thicken. Add the poppy seeds and process a few seconds more. Transfer to a small bowl and serve with the platter. Stir again just before serving.

(The Poppy-Seed Dressing can be made up to 3 days ahead and refrigerated.)

Cucumber, Garden Tomato, and Feta Salad

Serves 18

It's best to make this during tomato season, when many varieties are available—the different colors and shapes make it not just another salad.

1 large burpless unwaxed cucumber, sliced ¼ inch thick, unpeeled
1½ pounds Italian plum tomatoes, quartered
4 beefsteak or other large tomatoes (about 2 pounds), sliced ½ inch thick
1 large yellow tomato, sliced ½ inch thick, each slice then cut in half
2 pounds orange tomatoes, cut into wedges
1 pint basket yellow cherry or pear tomatoes (some cut in half, some left whole)
1 pint basket red cherry or pear tomatoes (some cut in half, some left whole)
1 small red onion, sliced paper thin
1 cup Kalamata olives
½ cup fresh mint leaves, packed
½ cup fresh basil leaves, packed
¾ cup extra-virgin olive oil
¼ cup white-wine vinegar
1 tablespoon salt
1 teaspoon freshly ground black pepper
¾ pound feta cheese, crumbled

In a large bowl, mix the cucumber, tomatoes, onion, olives, mint, and basil. Set aside.

In a small bowl, mix the olive oil, vinegar, salt, and pepper.

To serve, dress the salad, then transfer it to a serving platter and distribute the feta on top.

(You can have everything cut and ready to go the night before. Don't dress the salad until you are ready to serve it, as the dressing will extract the tomato juices and make the salad watery.)

Mocha-Cocoa-Nut Muffins

Makes about 36 muffins

Is this a muffin or an individual mocha-chocolate-nut cake? You'll feel less guilty if you think of it as a muffin. This recipe is adapted from *Morning Food*, by Margaret Fox. Best of all, it will yield enough so you'll have breakfast the next morning.

6 large eggs
1½ cups vegetable oil
2 cups buttermilk
1 cup strong coffee, preferably flavored (such as hazelnut)
2 teaspoons vanilla extract
3 cups all-purpose flour
2½ cups whole-wheat flour
2 cups dark-brown sugar, packed
2 teaspoons baking soda
1 teaspoon baking powder
2 teaspoons salt
⅔ cup Dutch-process cocoa (sift first, then measure)
2 cups chopped walnuts
2 cups semisweet chocolate chips or chunks

Preheat the oven to 350° F. Coat three 12-muffin pans with vegetable-oil cooking spray and set aside.

In a large bowl, mix the eggs, oil, buttermilk, coffee, and vanilla until well blended. Set aside.

In another large bowl, blend the two flours, brown sugar, baking soda, baking powder, salt, and cocoa. Stir in the walnuts and the chocolate chips. Pour the liquid mixture over the dry ingredients and stir until they are just combined; do not overmix.

Spoon the batter into the prepared pans so that each cup is ¾ full, and bake for 20 to 25 minutes, or until a cake tester inserted in the center comes out clean.

Remove the pans from the oven and let them cool on a rack for 15 minutes before inverting the muffins. Serve warm.

(The muffins can be made up to a month ahead and frozen. They are best served warm, so reheat them in a 325° F oven for 10 to 15 minutes.)

Apricot-Almond Loaf with Sweetened Goat Cheese

Makes two 9 × 5-inch loaves

Not only can this be served for brunch, but it also makes an excellent offering for a tea or dessert party. This recipe is an adaptation from *The Loaves and Fishes Party Cookbook*, by Anna Pump and Sybille Pump.

¾ pound (3 sticks) unsalted butter, at room temperature
2⅓ cups sugar
4 large eggs
Grated zest of 1 large lemon
1½ teaspoons almond extract
1½ cups milk
4 cups unbleached flour
4 teaspoons baking powder
1 cup slivered almonds
2 cups dried apricots, coarsely chopped
2 tablespoons apricot brandy (optional)
Sweetened Goat Cheese (recipe follows)

Preheat the oven to 350° F. Butter two 9 × 5-inch loaf pans.

In a large bowl with an electric mixer, cream the butter and the sugar. Beat in the eggs. Mix in the lemon zest, almond extract, and milk. Add the flour, baking powder, almonds, apricots, and brandy, and mix just to combine; don't overmix.

Divide the batter between the prepared loaf pans and bake for 1 hour, or until a cake tester inserted in the center comes out clean.

Remove the pans from the oven and let cool on a rack for 15 minutes before inverting the pans. Let the loaves cool to room temperature before slicing.

(These loaves can be made up to a month ahead and frozen.)

Sweetened Goat Cheese

Makes about 2½ cups

1 pound soft mild goat cheese
¼ cup confectioners' sugar
1¼ cups heavy cream
1 teaspoon freshly ground black pepper

In the bowl of a food processor fitted with the metal blade, process the goat cheese and sugar for a few seconds. Add the heavy cream and the pepper and process until fluffy, about 30 seconds more. Transfer the mixture to several small bowls and serve with the apricot bread.

The Lunch Party

Time to Serve: Between 11:30 A.M. and 2:30 P.M.

Warm Garlic Puffs

A New Niçoise

Freeform Puff-Pastry
Fruit Tart

These days, lunch is sadly becoming a lost art; most of us are in such a rush, we usually grab some fast-food concoction or end up skipping the meal altogether. This makes a lunch party all the more attractive; it's a natural break in the day, and you don't have to worry about guests lingering too long.

When planning a lunch menu, keep in mind that your time frame may be limited, especially if you're hosting a business lunch. People can usually block out no more than a couple of hours at the most on a weekday, so you should have lunch completely prepared by the time your guests arrive—the table should be set, beverages in order, and the cooking pretty much done.

Give yourself the time you need to set up for lunch. If you're doing it during a workday, set the table and prepare as much as you can the night before. If you have the leisure of doing it on a weekend, do your preparation the morning of the lunch.

Salads like this New Niçoise make for the perfect luncheon entree. Your guests will feel as though they're eating something healthful and light, and won't feel too guilty about indulging in luscious side dishes and desserts.

Lunch Party Menu—Serves 12

Warm Garlic Puffs
A New Niçoise
Buttermilk Cornbread
Freeform Puff-Pastry Fruit Tart

Warm Garlic Puffs

Makes 30 to 36 small puffs

These light, garlicky puffs are the perfect prelude to a lunch where the main course is a salad.

8 garlic cloves, peeled
½ cup water
½ teaspoon salt
Dash freshly ground black pepper
3 tablespoons unsalted butter
½ cup unbleached flour
2 large eggs

Preheat the oven to 400° F. Line a baking sheet with parchment paper and coat with vegetable-oil cooking spray.

Place the peeled garlic cloves in a small bowl, cover with plastic wrap, and microwave on high for 3 to 5 minutes, or until the garlic is soft. Remove from the oven and mash the garlic with a fork to make a paste.

Put the water, salt, pepper, and butter in a small saucepan and bring to a boil. Add the flour and stir continuously for about 2 minutes, or until the mixture pulls away from the sides of the pan.

Transfer the flour mixture to the bowl of an electric mixer. With the mixer running on medium speed, add the eggs one at a time; then add the garlic paste.

Put the dough in a pastry bag fitted with a large star tip. Pipe the puffs onto the prepared baking sheet in teaspoon-sized mounds. Bake 10 to 15 minutes, or until golden. Serve warm.

(You can make these puffs the day before; store in an airtight container and heat on a baking sheet at 300° F for 7 to 10 minutes.)

A New Niçoise

Serves 12

If you don't like swordfish, substitute tuna or salmon. Though filling, this salad will leave room for dessert. Don't be daunted by the length of this recipe—it's really very easy to prepare. If you positively cannot find quail eggs, you may substitute 6 chicken eggs.

12 small to medium beets
36 baby redskin potatoes
1½ pounds green beans, trimmed
2 dozen quail eggs
3 pounds mixed greens (radicchio, oakleaf,
     arugula, and frisée, or your own combination)
12 8-ounce swordfish steaks
¼ cup extra-virgin olive oil
1 teaspoon cinnamon
1 teaspoon cumin
1 tablespoon turmeric
Salt and freshly ground black pepper
½ pint yellow cherry or pear tomatoes
½ pint red cherry or pear tomatoes
Capers
Opal or green basil leaves
Pansies or other edible flowers
Citrus Dressing (recipe follows)

To prepare the beet flowers: Preheat the oven to 425° F. Wash and trim the beets. Wrap each beet in aluminum foil, place on a baking sheet, and bake for 1 hour. Remove from the oven, remove the foil, and, with cold water running over the beet, slip the skin off. After the beets are all skinned, make crosscuts in each beet 1 inch deep and ¼ inch apart. Gently pry the cuts apart with your fingers. Cover and set aside.

While the beets are baking, prepare the other cooked vegetables. Bring a large pot of water to a boil over high heat. Meanwhile, with a potato peeler, remove a strip of skin from each potato around its middle. Put the potatoes in the boiling water and cook for 10 to 15 minutes. You don't want them to fall apart, but they should be tender. Drain and set aside.

Bring a medium pot of water to a boil. Add the green beans and blanch for 3 minutes, or until crisp-tender. Drain the beans, then put them in ice water immediately and chill for 3 to 5 minutes until cold. Drain on paper towels and set aside.

Put the quail eggs in a small pan and cover with cold water. Bring to a boil over high heat and cook for 7 to 10 minutes, until hard-boiled. Drain, peel, and set aside.

Wash and dry the lettuces and set aside.

Brush the fish with the olive oil. Mix the cinnamon, cumin, and turmeric in a small bowl and sprinkle the mixture on both sides of the fish. Season the fish on both sides with salt and pepper, and let stand at room temperature for 30 minutes. Grill or broil the fish for about 5 minutes on each side, until it is firm. Set aside to serve at room temperature.

To assemble the salad, divide the lettuce among 12 plates and top with a piece of fish. Decorate each plate with a beet flower, 3 potatoes, a few green beans, 2 quail eggs (one cut in half) and some yellow and red cherry tomatoes. Garnish each salad with a few capers, basil leaves, and edible flowers. Serve with Citrus Dressing on the side.

Citrus Dressing

Makes 1½ cups

¼ cup fresh orange juice
¼ cup fresh lemon juice
1 teaspoon grated orange zest
1 teaspoon grated lemon zest
1 cup extra-virgin olive oil
Salt and freshly ground black pepper

In the bowl of a food processor fitted with the metal blade, process the juices and zests for a few seconds. With the motor running, add the olive oil in a thin stream until it is incorporated. Add salt and pepper to taste.

(You can make this dressing up to 2 days ahead and refrigerate.)

Buttermilk Cornbread

Makes one 4 × 12-inch loaf

This cornbread is very dense, and the honey and buttermilk flavors really come through. It is best served warm.

1½ cups unbleached flour
1½ cups fine yellow cornmeal
1½ tablespoons baking powder
2 teaspoons salt
3 large eggs
1½ cups buttermilk
3 tablespoons honey
6 tablespoons unsalted butter, melted
2 jalapeño peppers, seeded and finely chopped
2½ cups chopped green and red bell peppers

Preheat the oven to 400° F. Coat a 4 × 12-inch loaf pan with vegetable-oil cooking spray.

In a medium bowl, combine the flour, cornmeal, baking powder, and salt. In a larger bowl, combine the eggs, buttermilk, honey, and melted butter. Mix the dry ingredients into the liquid until well incorporated. Add the jalapeño and bell peppers and mix well. Pour the batter into the prepared pan and bake for 25 to 35 minutes, or until the loaf springs back when touched in the center.

(This can be made a week ahead and frozen. Remove from the freezer and thaw at room temperature about 2 hours before serving. Reheat in 300° F oven for 20 minutes until warmed through.)

Freeform Puff-Pastry Fruit Tart

Makes two 10-inch tarts

This tart is not too sugary, so the fruit really takes center stage. The slightly sweetened crème fraîche adds the perfect touch, and don't feel guilty eating it—you've watched your calories during lunch. We've used white nectarines, but peeled peaches would be great as well.

1 17¼-ounce package puff-pastry dough, thawed
10 medium ripe-yet-firm white nectarines
1 pint blueberries, rinsed and picked over
1 cup apple jelly
1 pint crème fraîche
½ cup confectioners' sugar, sifted

Preheat the oven to 350° F.

To make the tart shells, line the bottom of two 10-inch quiche or tart pans with parchment paper, then coat with vegetable-oil cooking spray. Roll the puff pastry ⅛ inch thick. Set the 10-inch pan on top of the pastry and cut around it with a knife to make two 12-inch circles. Place a circle of dough into each pan, letting the edges of the pastry fall over the sides. With your fingers, fold the overhanging pastry back onto itself, making sure that ¼ inch of the pastry rests on the rim of the pan, creating a freeform, wavy look.

Line each pastry shell with foil and weight with pie weights or dried beans. Bake for 15 to 20 minutes, until light gold in color. Remove the weights and foil, and bake about 10 minutes more, until the bottom is deep gold. Set aside to cool slightly.

Cut each unpeeled nectarine into eighths, and cover the bottom of each tart shell with the sliced fruit. (Arrange them in any way you wish.) Scatter the blueberries on top.

In a small saucepan set over low heat, melt the jelly. Brush the fruit carefully with the melted jelly.

Mix the crème fraîche with the confectioners' sugar. Cut each tart into six 8-inch wedges and serve with the sweetened crème fraîche on the side.

(Sweetened whipped cream or sour cream may be substituted for the crème fraîche.)

The Tea Party

Time to Serve: Between 3:00 and 5:00 P.M.

Open-Faced Radish-and-Cucumber Sandwiches, Red-Pepper Cream on Belgian Endive, and Basil Biscuits with Smoked Turkey and Cranberry Chutney

Smoked-Salmon Pinwheels

Whimsical Scones with Whipped Cream, Jam, and Lemon Curd, and Chocolate-Espresso Cookies

Tea Party Menu—Serves 20

Open-Faced Radish-and-Cucumber Sandwiches

Whimsical Scones with Whipped Cream, Jam, and Lemon Curd

Red-Pepper Cream on Belgian Endive

Smoked-Salmon Pinwheels

Basil Biscuits with Smoked Turkey and Cranberry Chutney

Trifle

Chocolate-Espresso Cookies

Candied Pecans

Tea parties conjure up images of the Mad Hatter and meals had at odd hours in foreign places. The ritual of stopping for tea, with its attendant goodies, has crept into the party repertoire, and it's a wonderful option for entertaining. This is an Old World custom to some, but it can be interpreted in many modern ways. Having a tea party is appropriate for birthdays, anniversaries, engagements, weddings, graduations—or just for tea.

One truism about tea parties: they can be a lot of work, especially if you prepare everything yourself. The petite sandwiches, scones, and biscuits, along with candied nuts, cookies, and perhaps even a wonderful trifle, require advance preparation and planning. Note, though, that many items can be made ahead of time, and I've indicated what can be done beforehand in the recipes. Even if you use store-bought items, remember to leave plenty of time before your party to arrange and present the various platters.

For a proper tea party, you'll need all the accouterments: teapots, cups, saucers, sugar bowls, cream pitchers, plates, platters, and other serving pieces. Don't forget linens. If you don't have enough matching china or linen, have fun mixing and matching things that you do have on hand, or borrow from friends. If you prefer everything to match, you can rent all the pieces you'll need from a party rental company. The nonfood components of your tea party can be done well in advance.

When your guests arrive, offer them a glass of sherry or champagne (non-alcoholic champagne or mineral water should be on hand for those who don't imbibe).

If you don't have enough tea strainers (and who does?) to brew several types of tea, perhaps offer only one favorite kind. Tea bags are another alternative; there are so many traditional and exotic varieties available that this is perfectly acceptable. If your party is held during a warm spell, you may wish to offer iced tea or homemade lemonade along with the hot tea. And don't forget the lemon wedges, honey, and sugar, as well as cream and milk.

Since your guests will most likely want to taste at least one of everything, make sure to provide for seconds. Allowances have been made for this in the recipes.

Open-Faced Radish-and-Cucumber Sandwiches

Makes 40 sandwiches

Cucumber sandwiches are classic to a tea menu; this version also has radish and peppery watercress.

1 bunch red radishes
10 slices white sandwich bread (preferably from a bakery)
¾ cup (1½ sticks) unsalted butter, softened
1 burpless unwaxed cucumber
1 bunch watercress, rinsed and dried

Scrub the radishes, place in cold water, and refrigerate for at least 30 minutes.

Cut the crusts off the bread. Butter each slice and cut into 4 squares.

Drain the radishes, then dry with paper towels. Slice each radish paper-thin. Slice the unpeeled cucumber paper-thin. Alternate slices of radish and cucumber on the buttered bread and garnish with watercress.

(These sandwiches can be made up to 4 hours ahead. Cover and refrigerate. Allow them to come to room temperature before serving.)

Whimsical Scones with Whipped Cream, Jam, and Lemon Curd

Makes 36 scones

You'd better not be on a no-fat diet if you want to eat one of these biscuity scones! If you wish, add ½ cup of currants or dried cherries to the dough just before kneading. Although these are great plain, they're heavenly with cream, jam, or this ultrarich and tart lemon curd. The scone and lemon curd recipes are adaptations from *Café Beaujolais*, by Margaret Fox.

4 cups unbleached flour
2 tablespoons sugar
2 tablespoons baking powder
½ cup (1 stick) unsalted butter, cut into 1-inch pieces and frozen
2¼ cups heavy cream

1 cup heavy whipped cream
Strawberry, blueberry, or raspberry jam
Lemon Curd (recipe follows)

Preheat the oven to 375° F. Line two baking sheets with parchment paper and coat with vegetable-oil cooking spray.

In the bowl of an electric mixer, combine the flour, sugar, and baking powder. Add the frozen butter pieces and blend at medium speed until the butter is broken up and evenly distributed.

Add two cups of the heavy cream and mix just to blend; the dough should look coarse, with small lumps of butter still visible.

Transfer the dough to a lightly floured board and knead about 8 times. Roll out ½ inch thick. Dip a whimsically shaped cookie cutter into some flour and cut out the dough. Knead the scraps 2 or 3 times, reroll, and repeat.

Place the scones on the prepared baking sheets and brush with the remaining ¼ cup of heavy cream. Bake for 20 to 25 minutes, or until golden brown. Remove to a rack and cool. Serve with whipped cream, jam, and Lemon Curd (recipe follows).

(These scones are best made the day of your tea.)

Lemon Curd

Makes 2 cups

3 large eggs
6 egg yolks
¾ cup sugar
Pinch salt
½ cup plus 1 tablespoon fresh lemon juice
3 tablespoons grated lemon zest
9 tablespoons unsalted butter

In the top of a double boiler set over medium heat, blend the eggs, egg yolks, sugar, salt, lemon juice, and lemon zest, whisking continuously, until thick, about 15 minutes. Do not let the bottom of the pan touch the water, and do not let the mixture come to a boil. Remove the double boiler from the heat. Add the butter piece by piece, whisking continuously, until it is all incorporated. Let cool completely, then refrigerate until ready to use.

(Lemon Curd can be made up to a month ahead and frozen.)

Red-Pepper Cream on Belgian Endive

Serves 20

Belgian endive is such an elegant green; the pale red of the pepper cream on the endive spears is a visual treat.

4 large red bell peppers
1 tablespoon tomato paste
8 ounces cream cheese, softened
2 tablespoons unsalted butter, softened
Salt
White pepper
3 to 4 large heads Belgian endive

Preheat the oven to 350° F.

Cut the peppers in half, rinse and seed them, and score the skin sides. Place them cut side down on a baking sheet and bake until soft, about 15 minutes. Transfer the peppers to the bowl of a food processor fitted with the metal blade. Add the tomato paste, and process for 2 to 3 minutes, or until puréed. Remove the mixture from the bowl and force it through a strainer to get rid of any remaining pepper skin; set aside.

Put the cream cheese and the butter in the bowl of the food processor and process until well blended. Add salt and pepper to taste, then add the red-pepper mixture and blend well. Transfer the creamed mixture to a bowl and refrigerate for at least 30 minutes.

Separate the endive into leaves, rinse, and pat dry.

To serve, remove the cream mixture from the refrigerator and let stand for 15 minutes to soften. Place the mixture in a pastry bag fitted with a decorative tip. Pipe the red-pepper cream onto the endive leaves, and arrange them on a platter by themselves or with other offerings.

(The red-pepper cream can be made up to 2 days ahead, but don't pipe it onto the endive leaves more than 45 minutes before serving, as the endive tends to dry up and curl at the edges.)

Smoked-Salmon Pinwheels

Makes 50 to 60 pieces

Dill-infused cream cheese and delicate smoked salmon are made for each other.

8 ounces cream cheese, softened
1 tablespoon chopped fresh dill (or more, to taste)
1 loaf unsliced white sandwich bread, cut lengthwise into 6 or 7 slices, each about ½ inch thick
1 pound smoked salmon, sliced (do not use lox)

In the bowl of a food processor fitted with the metal blade, combine the cream cheese and the dill, and process until soft and fluffy. Set aside.

Remove the crusts from the bread. With a long metal spatula, spread a thin layer of cream cheese on each slice of bread. Place about 2 ounces of salmon over half the length of each slice. Starting from the salmon side, roll up the slices, pressing down as you roll. Wrap each roll separately in plastic wrap, and refrigerate for at least 2 hours, or overnight.

To serve, remove the plastic wrap, and cut each roll at an angle into 10 to 12 slices. Arrange on a platter.

(The pinwheel rolls can be made the day before, but do not slice them until the day of the party. After slicing, cover and refrigerate up to 3 hours before serving.)

dry ingredients, rubbing with your fingers until the mixture forms coarse crumbs.

Stir the basil into the yogurt and add to the dry mixture, stirring with a wooden spoon until the yogurt is incorporated. Gather the dough into a ball, transfer to a lightly floured board, and knead until it holds together. Divide the dough into 20 pieces (about golf-ball size). Flatten the balls slightly and place ten of them onto each prepared pan. Melt the remaining 2 tablespoons of butter and brush the tops of the dough. Sprinkle with the remaining ¼ cup of Parmesan cheese. Bake for 30

Basil Biscuits with Smoked Turkey and Cranberry Chutney

Makes 20 biscuits

These biscuits are delicious even without this savory filling. If you prefer, substitute Black Forest ham or smoked chicken for the turkey. The biscuit recipe is adapted from *Sunset* magazine; the cranberry chutney, from an entertaining video by Martha Stewart.

4 cups unbleached flour
4 teaspoons baking powder
1 teaspoon baking soda
1¼ cups freshly grated Parmesan cheese
½ pound (2 sticks) unsalted butter, cold
⅔ cup chopped fresh basil, packed
1½ cups plain low-fat yogurt
1¾ pounds smoked turkey, thinly sliced
Cranberry Chutney (recipe follows)

Preheat the oven to 400° F. Coat two 9-inch cake pans with vegetable-oil cooking spray.

In a large bowl, mix the flour, baking powder, baking soda, and 1 cup of the Parmesan. Cut all but 2 tablespoons of the butter into small pieces and add it to the

Trifle

Candied Pecans

minutes, or until golden brown. Remove to a rack and let cool completely.

To assemble, split each biscuit. Spread a little Cranberry Chutney on each half, and top with about 1½ ounces (1 slice) turkey.

(Make these biscuits the day you're going to serve them. They can be assembled up to 1½ hours before serving. Cover with plastic wrap until ready to serve.)

Cranberry Chutney

Makes 1 quart

3¼ cups sugar
¾ cup water
2 oranges, peeled and cut into cubes
1½ lemons, peeled and cut into cubes
2-inch piece of gingerroot, peeled and minced
1½ cups raisins
1 vanilla bean
2 cinnamon sticks
3½ pounds fresh cranberries, rinsed

In a large saucepan set over medium-high heat, combine the sugar and water and cook until the sugar has melted, about 5 minutes, stirring continuously. Add the orange and lemon cubes, minced gingerroot, raisins, vanilla bean, cinnamon sticks, and cranberries, and cook until thick, about 15 minutes, stirring 3 or 4 times. Remove from the heat and let cool. Remove the cinnamon sticks and vanilla bean and discard. Place in a glass container and refrigerate.

(This can be made up to 2 weeks ahead and refrigerated.)

Trifle

Serves 20

Trifle is a great addition to a tea menu—and not just because it is traditionally English. Much of it can be made in advance, and the rest of it finished just before serving.

4 cups milk, scalded
⅔ cup granulated sugar
Pinch salt
8 large egg yolks, slightly beaten
2 teaspoons vanilla extract

2 pints strawberries
1 pint blueberries
1 pint raspberries
1 pound black plums, pitted
1 pound peaches, pitted
2 small bunches red seedless grapes
½ cup cream sherry
½ cup fresh orange juice
2 16-ounce all-butter pound cakes

2 cups heavy cream
1 teaspoon vanilla extract
½ cup confectioners' sugar
Mint leaves

First, make the custard: In the top of a double boiler set over medium heat, combine the scalded milk, granulated sugar, and salt, stirring until the sugar dissolves. Add the egg yolks and stir constantly until the mixture thickens, about 5 minutes. Remove from the heat, stir in the vanilla, and let cool.

Next, prepare the fruit: Clean and cut the fruit as you would for a fruit salad (reserving ½ cup of the blueberries, 1 bunch of the grapes, and about 5 strawberries, stems intact). Mix and set aside.

In a small bowl, combine the sherry and the orange juice.

Cut each pound cake lengthwise into 9 slices, about ½-inch thick, then cut the slices in half, so that each piece is 3 × 6 inches.

Now, assemble the trifle: Cover the bottom of a clear 4-quart glass bowl with 2 slices of cake, then layer slices of cake, overlapping, all the way around the sides of the bowl. Sprinkle the cake with some of the sherry mixture.

Spread a 1-inch-thick layer of the cooled custard on the cake at the bottom. Next, add a 1-inch layer of the mixed fruit. Then add a few slices of the cake, drizzling it with the sherry mixture. Repeat until you are ½ inch from the top of the bowl. The final layer of cake should be no higher than the overlapping slices lining your bowl.

Just before serving, whip the cream to stiff peaks with the vanilla and the confectioners' sugar. Spread a generous layer of whipped cream on top of the trifle, and decorate with the reserved fruit and mint leaves.

(You can assemble the trifle, minus the whipped cream, the morning of the party, and refrigerate it.)

Chocolate-Espresso Cookies

Makes about sixty 1½-inch cookies

This is like having a demitasse of espresso and a good piece of chocolate at the same time. These little morsels are no more than two bites, but they are two bites of heaven. They'll become part of your permanent recipe repertoire.

¼ pound (1 stick) unsalted butter
4 ounces unsweetened chocolate, chopped
3 cups semisweet chocolate chips (about 18 ounces)
4 large eggs, at room temperature
½ cup sugar
2 tablespoons freeze-dried-espresso granules
1 teaspoon vanilla extract
½ cup flour
½ teaspoon baking powder
½ teaspoon salt

Preheat the oven to 350° F. Line a baking sheet with parchment paper and coat with vegetable-oil cooking spray.

In a medium saucepan set over low heat, melt the butter, unsweetened chocolate, and ½ cup of the chocolate chips, stirring to combine. Remove from the heat and let cool slightly.

In a large bowl, beat the eggs and the sugar until pale yellow. Stir in the coffee granules and the vanilla. Fold the melted-chocolate mixture into the egg mixture. Stir in the flour, baking powder, and salt. Add the remaining chocolate chips, and stir to distribute. Cover the bowl with plastic wrap and refrigerate for 15 minutes.

Drop the dough onto the prepared baking sheet by the teaspoonful. Bake for 10 to 12 minutes, or until the tops look cracked. Remove the cookies to a rack and cool completely. Store in an airtight container.

(These cookies freeze really well, up to 1 month.)

Candied Pecans

Makes about 6 cups

Sweet and spicy—bet you can't eat just one! If you have any left, put these in a special container and present them to a friend for a wonderful gift.

1½ pounds pecan halves
1 cup sugar
6 tablespoons vegetable oil
1 tablespoon cinnamon
2 tablespoons paprika
½ teaspoon cumin
½ teaspoon cayenne pepper (or to taste)
1 teaspoon salt

Preheat the oven to 250° F.

Bring 3 quarts of water to a boil in a large saucepan. Add the pecans and cook for 3 minutes. Drain, and transfer the pecans to a bowl. Sprinkle immediately with the sugar and mix well.

In a large nonstick skillet set over medium-high heat, heat the oil. Lower the heat to medium, add the pecans, and cook, stirring constantly, for 10 to 15 minutes, or until the nuts begin to separate. Spread the nuts on a baking sheet and bake for 25 to 30 minutes, or until crispy.

Meanwhile, combine the cinnamon, paprika, cumin, cayenne, and salt in a small bowl. Remove the nuts from the oven. Sprinkle the spice mixture over the hot nuts. Let cool before storing.

(These will keep for 1 week, stored in an airtight container.)

Pizzas with Eggplant
and Yellow
Tomatoes

Sweet-Potato
Pancakes with Sour
Cream and Golden
Caviar

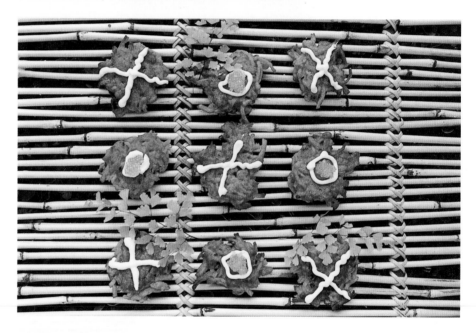

Marinated Olives and fresh Mozzarella

The Cocktail Party

Time to Serve: Between 6:00 and 8:00 P.M.

Cocktail parties are a wonderful way to entertain a group of any size. While they can be small and intimate, they're ideal for entertaining large groups, especially if you lack adequate seating or space for a sizable sit-down dinner, or would like to have a more varied guest list than you can successfully pull together at a smaller party.

Since they usually take place at the end of the workday, generally between six and eight in the evening, cocktail parties (which are sometimes called hors d'oeuvres or appetizer parties) are gatherings that give guests a chance to mingle and chat in a relaxed yet energized atmosphere. They also allow you, as the host, to serve small tastes of delicious food—lots of which can easily be prepared well ahead of time.

There are several ways to plan a cocktail party: the hors d'oeuvres can be passed, they can be set up on tables where guests can help themselves, or you can do both. The bottom line is ease and comfort; everyone should enjoy a cocktail party, including the host and hostess.

"Bite-sized" is one of the most important terms in the cocktail-party lexicon. You want to offer just a nibble or two—of delectable morsels. Not only are large portions unwieldy at a cocktail party, but guests feel too full too fast. Keep in mind that many of your guests will be having dinner afterward, and that your largesse should be in the form of conviviality and teasing tastes of interesting flavors, rather than in the size of the portions.

Planning the menu for a cocktail party is a great deal of fun—this kind of party really gives you a chance to let your imagination run free. This is your chance to make all those dishes from that drawer full of cut-out recipes, or to make an eclectic mix of your favorites. Perhaps you'd like to build your party around an ethnic-food theme—Asian, Latin, Italian, or Middle Eastern—and go on from there.

If you plan to have food passed on trays, you'll want to enlist extra help. Help may also be necessary for large stationary cocktail parties, since you'll need someone to make sure that the appetizers are continually replenished, and that they look fresh and appealing.

If you're serving passed hors d'oeuvres, make sure that guests are offered a napkin along with each appetizer. For a stationary appetizer table, be sure to provide lots of plates and forks, along with a generous supply of napkins. Food served at a buffet should require only one utensil, ideally a fork. Anything demanding a knife gets too complicated; guests should not have to worry about juggling eating implements. The importance of plates was made very clear at a cocktail party at which

When planning your cocktail party, you should figure on at least five paper cocktail napkins per guest.

Passed Hors d'Oeuvres—Serves 24

Pizzas with Eggplant and Yellow Tomatoes

Sweet-Potato Pancakes
with Sour Cream and Golden Caviar

Smoked-Salmon Tartare on Endive Leaves

Asian Spiced Shrimp

Polenta Crostini with Mushroom Marmalade

Stationary near the bar:
Marinated Olives and Fresh Mozzarella

none were to be found: one guest nonchalantly pulled a paper plate out of her purse—obviously, a veteran of such events.

If you decide to go with a buffet, bear in mind that the more foods you can serve at room temperature, the better. This means lower maintenance and fewer lags in replenishing the food, as you don't have to run back and forth, keeping things hot or cold, and bringing them out at the right temperature.

Unless the party is small, you'll probably want to hire a bartender. Serving drinks yourself works best if you're offering only wine, champagne, beer, and other low-maintenance beverages. If you plan to have more than a dozen guests or offer a full bar, you'll have a better time if a professional handles the mixology.

We've created two cocktail-party menus; both serve 24. The passed hors d'oeuvres menu is substantial, yet not too heavy. Our appetizer buffet menu offers a colorful combination of eclectic tastes and textures.

A practical—and beautiful—way to display dips and sauces is to use hollow vegetables or fruits as bowls, as we have for the Plum-Mustard Dip on page 122. Ceramic vegetable or fruit bowls, as we've used for the aïoli and peanut dips, work nicely, too. Garnish trays with leaves and flowers from your garden. (Remember to wash them.)

Beverages

For your cocktail party, you can offer either a full bar or just wine or champagne and mineral waters. You may also want to serve cocktails like martinis, daiquiris, and margaritas. Rose-colored martinis, tinted with a splash of Campari, are both beautiful and intriguingly flavored. And, as always, have nonalcoholic drinks available.

Pizzas with Eggplant and Yellow Tomatoes

Makes 40 to 50 appetizer-sized wedges

Though there are several different types of ready-made pizza crusts, the Boboli brand works best for this recipe. If you're pressed for time, substitute store-bought tomato sauce for homemade.

¼ cup vegetable oil
4 medium Japanese eggplant, sliced ¾ inch thick
5 7-inch prepared pizza crusts
Tomato Sauce, about ½ cup per pizza (recipe follows)
2 cups (1 pound) freshly shredded mozzarella cheese
1 pint yellow cherry tomatoes, halved (red cherry tomatoes may be substituted)
Fresh basil leaves

Preheat the oven to 400° F. Coat a baking sheet with vegetable-oil cooking spray.

In a large nonstick skillet set over medium heat, heat the oil. Add the eggplant slices and sauté on each side until golden brown, about 5 minutes per side. Remove the eggplant from the skillet, drain on paper towels, and set aside.

Spread each pizza crust with tomato sauce. Sprinkle with the mozzarella, and top with the halved tomatoes and the eggplant slices. Bake each pizza on a prepared cookie sheet for 10 to 15 minutes, or until the cheese is bubbly. Remove from the oven and let cool for 2 minutes before cutting into 8 to 10 slices. Garnish with fresh basil leaves.

(These can be assembled the day before and baked just before serving. Bake them 2 at a time and serve hot from the oven.)

Tomato Sauce

Makes 2 cups

2 tablespoons extra-virgin olive oil
1 small yellow onion, chopped
4 garlic cloves, minced
1 12–14-ounce can whole tomatoes
½ teaspoon dried oregano
Salt
Freshly ground black pepper

In a large nonstick skillet set over medium-high heat, heat the oil. Add the chopped onion and cook until translucent, about 5 minutes. Add the garlic and cook, stirring, for a few seconds. Add the tomatoes with their juice and the oregano. Cook over medium heat for 30 to 35 minutes, until thick. Add salt and pepper to taste. Let cool to room temperature.

Transfer the sauce to the bowl of a food processor fitted with the metal blade. Process for 30 seconds to 1 minute, or until smooth.

(The sauce can be refrigerated for up to 3 days or frozen for up to 1 month.)

Sweet-Potato Pancakes with Sour Cream and Golden Caviar

Makes about 60 1½–2-inch pancakes

Almost everyone loves potato pancakes, served plain or with sour cream. This gingered sweet-potato version is a real winner. Choose the caviar according to your budget.

2 pounds sweet potatoes
2 large eggs, lightly beaten
¼ cup unbleached flour
¼ cup gingersnap crumbs
1-inch piece gingerroot, peeled and grated

1 tablespoon chopped scallion (green part only)
1 teaspoon salt
½ teaspoon freshly ground black pepper
½ cup vegetable oil
1 cup sour cream or crème fraîche
4 ounces golden or other caviar

Peel the sweet potatoes and shred them in a food processor fitted with the coarse shredding disk, or with a hand grater. Transfer the shredded potatoes to a large bowl. Add the eggs, and mix with a spoon. Stir in the flour, cookie crumbs, ginger, scallions, salt, and pepper.

In a large nonstick skillet set over medium heat, heat 1 tablespoon of the vegetable oil. Drop the potato batter by the tablespoonful into the skillet, and cook on both sides until golden brown, about 2 minutes per side. Drain on paper towels. Add additional oil to the skillet to cook each batch.

When ready to serve, reheat the pancakes on a cookie sheet in a 300° F oven for 7 to 10 minutes, or until warmed through. Put the sour cream or crème fraîche into a squeeze bottle to apply to the pancakes. Place ¼ teaspoon of sour cream or crème fraîche on each pancake and garnish with a dab of caviar. Arrange on a tray or basket and serve at once.

(Once the batter has been mixed, the pancakes must be cooked immediately. They can be made up to 6 hours ahead and warmed through before serving.)

Smoked-Salmon Tartare on Endive Leaves

60 teaspoon-sized portions

With all the health concerns about raw fish, using smoked salmon for a tartare makes sense.

1 pound smoked salmon, sliced thin and then chopped
1 tablespoon chopped fresh dill
1 medium red onion, finely chopped
12 chives, chopped
1 teaspoon Dijon mustard
1 tablespoon capers, chopped
1 tablespoon extra-virgin olive oil
2 teaspoons fresh lemon juice
4 large heads Belgian endive

In a medium bowl, mix the salmon, dill, onion, chives, mustard, capers, olive oil, and lemon juice.

Separate the endive into leaves, rinse, and pat dry. Place a teaspoonful of the salmon mixture onto each leaf, arrange on a serving tray, and serve at once.

(The salmon tartare can be made a day in advance; cover with plastic wrap and refrigerate. Don't assemble these more than 45 minutes before serving, as the endive tends to dry and curl at the edges.)

Smoked-Salmon Tartare
on Endive Leaves

Polenta Crostini with Mushroom Marmalade

Asian Spiced Shrimp

Asian Spiced Shrimp

Makes about 50 to 60 shrimps

Shrimp is a luxury and will almost always be a costly addition to your party budget. This dish, however, is well worth the expense; the intense seasonings infuse the shrimp with complex and wonderful flavors.

3 pounds medium (16 to 20 per pound) shrimp, in the shell
2 tablespoons minced garlic
1 tablespoon cumin
1½ tablespoons ground coriander
1½ teaspoons cayenne pepper
½ cup chopped scallion (green part only)
¾ cup chopped flat-leaf parsley
2-inch piece gingerroot, peeled and grated
2 tablespoons grated lemon zest
½ cup fresh lemon juice
¾ cup extra-virgin olive oil
Salt

Shell the shrimp, leaving on the tails, then devein and butterfly them.

In a large bowl, mix the garlic, cumin, coriander, cayenne, scallions, parsley, gingerroot, lemon zest, lemon juice, and olive oil; add salt to taste. Add the shrimp and stir until they are well coated. Cover and refrigerate for 24 hours, stirring occasionally.

In a large nonstick skillet set over medium heat, sauté the shrimp, about 12 or 13 at a time, for 2 to 3 minutes on each side, or until they turn pink. Remove and drain on paper towels. Repeat with the rest of the shrimp.

Arrange on a serving tray or in a basket, and serve at room temperature. Don't leave the shrimp out more than 5 hours.

(Cook these the same day you plan to serve them.)

Polenta Crostini with Mushroom Marmalade

Makes about 60 crostini

These crostini are a marvelous base for your favorite toppings. If the mushroom marmalade isn't to your taste, you can top them with sausage and peppers, or with grilled vegetables.

5 cups water
1 cup milk
4 tablespoons (½ stick) unsalted butter
1 tablespoon salt
2½ cups coarse yellow cornmeal
½ cup freshly grated Parmesan cheese
½ cup extra-virgin olive oil
Mushroom Marmalade (recipe follows)

Coat an 11 × 17-inch jelly-roll pan with vegetable-oil cooking spray.

In a large saucepan set over medium-high heat, combine the water, milk, butter, and salt, and bring to a boil. Add the cornmeal in a thin, steady stream, stirring constantly with a wooden spoon. Reduce the heat to low and cook for 15 to 20 minutes, stirring constantly. When the cornmeal mixture begins to pull away from the sides of the pot, stir in the Parmesan cheese.

Spread the polenta evenly on the prepared baking sheet, and let cool completely. Then cut into 1½–2-inch diamonds.

In a large nonstick skillet set over medium heat, heat 1 tablespoon of the oil. Brown the polenta diamonds on both sides, taking care that they do not touch, about 3 to 4 minutes per side or until golden. Drain on paper towels and set aside. Arrange on a platter or tray and serve warm, topped with a teaspoon of Mushroom Marmalade.

(The crostini can be made the morning of the party. Do not refrigerate the cooked polenta, as the texture will change. Warm in a 350° F oven for 5 minutes before adding the topping.)

Mushroom Marmalade

Makes about 2 cups

2 tablespoons extra-virgin olive oil
3 medium yellow onions, thinly sliced
1 tablespoon fresh thyme leaves, chopped
1 teaspoon salt
¼ teaspoon freshly ground black pepper
2 pounds button mushrooms, trimmed and sliced

In a large nonstick skillet set over medium-high heat, heat 1 tablespoon of the olive oil. Add the onions and cook until golden, about 15 minutes. Stir in the thyme, salt, and pepper, and remove from heat and transfer to a bowl.

In the same skillet, set over high heat, heat the remaining 1 tablespoon of olive oil. Add the sliced mushrooms. Cook until the liquid from the mushrooms evaporates and they look golden, about 10 to 15 minutes. Add the onion mixture to the mushrooms and cook over low heat 5 to 7 minutes more. Serve warm.

(This can be made up to 4 days in advance and refrigerated, or 2 weeks in advance and frozen; reheat before serving.)

Marinated Olives and Fresh Mozzarella

Makes 1 quart

This is a fabulous nibble to serve with drinks.

8 large garlic cloves, minced
4 fresh or dried bay leaves
½ cup fresh basil leaves, packed
1 cup extra-virgin olive oil
1 cup white-wine tarragon vinegar
½ teaspoon salt
1 teaspoon freshly ground black pepper
3 pounds fresh mozzarella balls (about 18 1-inch bocconcini, halved)
2 cups Kalamata olives

In a medium bowl, mix the garlic, bay leaves, basil, olive oil, vinegar, salt, and pepper. Add the mozzarella and the olives. Cover with plastic wrap and let marinate in the refrigerator for at least 24 hours, and up to 1 week.

Serve in bowls with toothpicks and a bowl for olive pits nearby.

Rosemary Roasted Walnuts

Grilled Carrots with Peanut Sauce

Grilled Asparagus with Lemon Aïoli

Basil, Sun-Dried Tomato, and Cheese Torta with Garlic Toasts

Caviar Painting

Wonton Chips with Plum-Mustard Dip

Santa Fe Sushi

Minced-Turkey Morsels with Tomato Chutney

Minted Melon Balls

Rosemary Roasted
Walnuts

Basil, Sun-Dried Tomato, and Cheese Torta with Garlic Toasts

Grilled Carrots with Peanut Sauce and Grilled Asparagus with Lemon Aïoli

Roasted Rosemary Walnuts

Makes about 1½ quarts

Fresh rosemary adds an aromatic note and pungent flavor to these nuts.

1½ pounds walnut halves (the largest you can find)
1 tablespoon extra-virgin olive oil
Salt
½ cup fresh rosemary leaves, plus branches for garnish

Preheat the oven to 250° F.

In a large bowl, mix the walnuts with the olive oil until the nuts are well coated. Salt to taste, then add the rosemary leaves. Spread the walnuts on a baking sheet in one layer and bake for 30 to 45 minutes, or until golden but not browned. Add more salt if necessary. Remove from the oven and let cool to room temperature.

Serve the nuts in baskets or bowls, and garnish with fresh rosemary branches.

(These can be made the day before; store them in an airtight container after they've cooled completely.)

Grilled Carrots with Peanut Sauce

Makes 90 to 100 pieces

It will probably take you longer to find the Thai chili sauce than to make this zesty Peanut Sauce—that's how easy the recipe is. As for the carrots, buy the biggest ones you can find. They take on a very sweet taste after grilling and are often mistaken for sweet potatoes.

10 to 12 jumbo carrots (about 5 to 6 pounds)
¼ cup extra-virgin olive oil
Peanut Sauce (recipe follows)

Peel the carrots and cut them at an angle into ¼-inch slices. Put them in a large bowl, drizzle with the olive oil, mix well, and set aside.

Prepare a charcoal grill and wait until the coals are white and there are no flames. (If you are using a gas grill, it should be set on medium heat.) Grill the carrots on both sides for about 2 to 3 minutes on each side, or just until they have grill marks on them. Drain on paper towels.

(If you don't have a grill, blanch the carrots for 1 to 2 minutes in boiling water, then plunge them into ice water and drain on paper towels; or roast them in a 400° F oven for 20 minutes.)

Serve the carrots in a basket or on a platter with Peanut Sauce.

Peanut Sauce

Makes about 2 cups

1 8-ounce jar salted dry-roasted peanuts
1 12-ounce bottle Thai sweet chili sauce (available in Thai markets and some supermarkets)
2 tablespoons Asian toasted-sesame oil
2 to 3 tablespoons water

In the bowl of a food processor fitted with the metal blade, combine the peanuts, chili sauce, and sesame oil. Process for 30 to 60 seconds, or until the peanuts are smooth. With the motor running, add the water a little at a time, until the sauce is the consistency of mayonnaise.

(You can make this up to a week in advance. Refrigerate until ready to use. Let it come to room temperature before serving.)

Grilled Asparagus with Lemon Aïoli

Serves 24

These grilled asparagus are perfect for those who are watching calories. They take on a wonderfully smoky taste after grilling. Your guests not counting calories will love the Lemon Aïoli. It is also delicious with other grilled vegetables, or with grilled fish.

3 to 4 pounds ½-inch-thick asparagus spears

Cut off the asparagus ends and discard. Rinse the asparagus, pat dry, and set aside.

Prepare a charcoal grill and wait until the coals are white and there are no flames. (If you are using a gas grill, it should be set on medium heat.) Grill the asparagus for about 5 minutes, or until they have grill marks on them, turning twice.

(If you don't have a grill, blanch the asparagus for 1 to 2 minutes in boiling water and then plunge them into ice water. Drain on paper towels.)

Arrange the asparagus on a platter or tray and serve with the Lemon Aïoli.

Lemon Aïoli

Makes 1¾ cups

1 tablespoon Dijon mustard
1 tablespoon minced garlic
6 tablespoons fresh lemon juice
2 egg yolks*
¾ cup extra-virgin olive oil
¾ cup vegetable oil
½ teaspoon grated lemon zest
1 teaspoon salt
½ teaspoon ground white pepper

In the bowl of a food processor fitted with the metal blade, combine the mustard, garlic, lemon juice, and egg yolks. Process for a few seconds.

Combine the olive and vegetable oils in a 2-cup measure. With the motor running on low, add the oil to the egg mixture in a thin, steady stream. Turn off the machine and add the lemon zest, salt, and pepper. Process a few seconds more. The aïoli should be thick, like mayonnaise.

Although this recipe calls for uncooked eggs, the U.S. Department of Agriculture has found them to be a potential carrier of food-borne illnesses, and recommends that diners avoid eating them. Egg substitutes may be used instead; check packages for equivalents.

Basil, Sun-Dried Tomato, and Cheese Torta with Garlic Toasts

Serves 24

This layered torta is the perfect cheese offering for an appetizer buffet spread. If you have enough left over after your party, mix ¾ to 1 cup of the torta with a pound of your favorite pasta for a delicious and easy dish.

3 pounds cream cheese, softened
¼ pound (1 stick) unsalted butter, softened
½ cup freshly grated Parmesan cheese
1 tablespoon dried thyme
1 tablespoon minced garlic
1 teaspoon salt
½ teaspoon ground white pepper

3 cups fresh basil leaves
6 garlic cloves, minced
½ cup pine nuts
¼ cup extra-virgin olive oil
1 teaspoon fresh lemon juice

Wonton Chips with Plum-Mustard Dip

Caviar Painting

Santa Fe Sushi

½ teaspoon salt
½ teaspoon freshly ground black pepper
¼ cup freshly grated Parmesan cheese

1½ cups sun-dried tomatoes
2 cups hot water
½ cup pine nuts
8 garlic cloves, minced
¼ cup extra-virgin olive oil
½ teaspoon salt
½ teaspoon freshly ground black pepper
¼ cup freshly grated Parmesan cheese

Garlic Toasts (recipe follows)

First put the sun-dried tomatoes to soak in 2 cups of hot water until softened, about 30 minutes.

Meanwhile, make the cream cheese mixture. In the bowl of a food processor fitted with the metal blade, combine the cream cheese and the butter, and process until soft, about 30 seconds. Add the Parmesan, thyme, garlic, salt, and pepper, and process a few seconds more. Transfer the mixture to a bowl and set aside.

Next, make the basil pesto: In the bowl of a food processor fitted with the metal blade, combine the basil, garlic, pine nuts, olive oil, lemon juice, salt, and pepper, and process until smooth, about 2 minutes. Add the Parmesan and process a few seconds more. Transfer the mixture to a bowl and set aside.

Next, make the sun-dried tomato pesto. Remove the softened tomatoes from the water and squeeze out the liquid. In the bowl of a food processor fitted with the metal blade, combine the tomatoes, pine nuts, garlic, olive oil, salt, and pepper, and process until smooth, about 2 minutes. Add the Parmesan and process a few seconds more. Transfer the mixture to a bowl and set aside.

Now, assemble the torta: Line the inside of a 2-quart glass or metal bowl with plastic wrap. Put a 2½-inch-thick layer of the cream-cheese mixture in the bottom of the bowl. Add a ½-inch-thick layer of sun-dried-tomato pesto, extending it evenly to the sides of the mold. Add a 2½-inch-thick layer of the cheese mixture, extending it evenly to the sides of the mold. Add a ½-inch-thick layer of the basil pesto, extending it evenly to the sides of the mold. Repeat until you reach the top of the mold, ending with a layer of the cream cheese. Fold the ends of the plastic wrap over the top of the mold to cover, and press down with your hand to compress the mold. Refrigerate for at least 6 hours, or until the torta is firm. Unmold onto a serving platter and surround with Herb Toasts.

(The torta can be made up to 2 days in advance. Unmold it just before serving.)

Garlic Toasts

Makes about 75 toasts

2 baguettes
1 cup extra-virgin olive oil
12 garlic cloves, minced
1 teaspoon paprika

Preheat the oven to 300° F. Cut the bread into slices ¼ to ½-inch thick.

In a small bowl, blend the olive oil, garlic, and paprika. Brush both sides of each slice of bread with the mixture. Bake on a cookie sheet for about 25 to 30 minutes, or until crisp and golden. Place the toasts around the torta or in a napkin-lined basket on the side.

(The toasts can be made a day ahead; store in an airtight container. If you wish, substitute your favorite crackers.)

Caviar Painting

Serves 24

Whether you do a Picasso face as we've done here, a Mondrian-like abstract design, or a Van Gogh sunflower, it's great fun to create an edible work of art out of caviar. You don't have to use expensive caviar for this dish, but don't use lumpfish caviar, as the colors will run.

3 pounds cream cheese, softened
1 pound (4 sticks) unsalted butter
4 ounces black caviar
8 ounces golden caviar

16 ounces red caviar
¼ cup black olives, pitted
2 12-ounce packages assorted biscuit crackers

In a large bowl, cream the cream cheese and the butter. Spread a 1-inch-thick layer of the mixture onto a 9 × 13-inch board or flat serving plate, leaving a ¼-inch border. Cover with plastic wrap and refrigerate for 2 hours.

With a small knife, lightly carve the outlines of a design or shape into the creamed mixture. Leave at least ¼ inch of the mixture intact on the bottom, and leave spaces between the elements of the patterns, so that the different colors of the caviar don't run. Fill in the outlines with the caviar, and decorate with olives.

Frame your piece of art with crackers.

(You can make the creamed background up to 2 days before and refrigerate. Fill in the caviar the morning of your party, and refrigerate until ready to serve.)

Wonton Chips with Plum-Mustard Dip

Serves 24

A new twist for those who love chip and dip.

Vegetable oil
2 10-ounce packages wonton skins
Plum-Mustard Dip (recipe follows)

Fill a wok or deep skillet about half full with oil, about 2½ to 3 inches deep, and heat over high flame. Reduce the heat to medium high. Drop the wonton skins in the oil, a few at a time, taking care that they do not touch. Cook until the wontons puff up and turn golden, about 1 to 2 minutes. Remove, drain on paper towels, and repeat until all the wontons are cooked. Serve with Plum-Mustard Dip.

Plum-Mustard Dip

Makes 2 cups

1½ cups plum sauce (available in the Oriental section of supermarkets)
½ cup Pommery or grainy mustard

In a small bowl, mix the plum sauce and the mustard until well blended.

Cover with plastic wrap and refrigerate until ready to serve. Transfer to a serving bowl and serve with the wonton chips.

(You can make the chips the day before; store them in an airtight container. The dip can also be made the day before, and refrigerated.)

Santa Fe Sushi

Makes 50 to 60 pieces

These tortilla roll-ups look like sushi, but they're made without fish and have a Southwestern flair.

1½ cups uncooked black beans
4 slices bacon
1½ teaspoons salt
2 large whole chicken breasts
3 large red bell peppers
2 bunches spinach
4 tablespoons (½ stick) unsalted butter
1 teaspoon cumin
Salt
5 12-inch flour tortillas

Rinse and pick over the beans. Place in a medium stockpot and add cold water to 2 inches above the beans. Add the bacon and the salt, and bring to a boil over high heat. Reduce the heat to low, cover, and cook until the beans are very soft, about 1½ hours.

While the beans are cooking, place the chicken breasts in a medium pot, add water to cover, and boil for about 15 to 20 minutes, or until the chicken is cooked through. Remove the chicken from the water and let cool. Remove and discard the bones and the skin, and cut the chicken into strips about ½-inch wide. Set aside.

Preheat the oven to 450° F. Cut the peppers in half, seed them, and clean them. Place the peppers, skin side up, on a baking sheet and cook for 30 minutes, or until they are soft and the skin begins to turn brown. Remove from the oven and place the peppers in a plastic bag, closing it with a twist-tie. Let cool for 5 minutes, then peel off the skins and cut the peppers into strips about ½ inch wide. Set aside.

Remove the stems from the spinach and wash well. Bring water to a boil in a large stockpot set over high heat, and blanch the spinach for 5 seconds, or until the color changes. Drain the spinach in a colander and rinse with cold water. Wait a few minutes, then squeeze any remaining water from the spinach with your hands or paper towels.

Drain the beans, reserving about ¼ cup of the liquid. Discard the bacon. In the bowl of a food processor fitted with the metal blade combine beans, butter, and cumin, and process into a paste. Add 2 to 3 tablespoons of the bean liquid if the mixture is too stiff. Add salt to taste.

To make the rolls, place each tortilla on a piece of plastic wrap. Across the center of each tortilla, place a ½-inch-wide strip of chicken; below that, a ½-inch-wide strip of red pepper; and below that, a ¼-inch-wide strip of spinach; finish with a ½-inch-wide strip of black bean paste.

Starting from below the beans, roll the tortilla tightly. When you reach the top, use a ¼-inch-wide strip of black bean paste to seal the roll. Wrap the rolls in plastic and refrigerate overnight. Just before serving, cut into slices ¾- to 1-inch thick.

(You can make the rolls up to 2 days before you plan to serve them.)

Minced-Turkey Morsels with Tomato Chutney

Makes 80 to 90 1½-inch fritters

These morsels are on the spicy side; paired with the Tomato Chutney, they are delicious.

2 large eggs
1½ cups milk
1½ cups bread crumbs
1 teaspoon turmeric
1 teaspoon curry powder
2 teaspoons minced garlic
2 teaspoons salt
½ teaspoon freshly ground black pepper
2 pounds ground turkey
½ cup vegetable oil
Tomato Chutney (recipe follows)

In a large bowl combine the eggs, milk, bread crumbs, turmeric, curry, garlic, salt, and pepper, and mix well. Add the turkey and mix as you would a meat loaf, by hand or with a wooden spoon.

In a large nonstick skillet set over medium heat, heat 1 tablespoon of the oil. Drop the turkey mixture into the skillet by the tablespoon. Cook on both sides until brown, about 5 minutes, then drain on paper towels. Repeat until all the turkey is cooked.

Serve at room temperature, or reheat in a 300° F oven for 10 minutes, until warmed through.

(These can be made the day before and reheated.)

Tomato Chutney

Makes about 1 quart

This recipe is an adaptation from *A Taste of India*, by Madhur Jaffrey. The secret ingredient here is panchphoran, a mixture of 5 Indian spices.

6 tablespoons vegetable oil

1½ teaspoons panchphoran (available at Indian markets)

3-inch piece fresh gingerroot, peeled and cut into matchsticks

5 small dried whole red chilies

2 tablespoons chopped garlic

3 pounds Italian plum tomatoes, cut into 8 wedges

3 teaspoons salt

¾ cup sugar

½ cup dried apricots, thinly sliced

6 fresh whole jalapeño peppers, stems intact

In a large nonstick skillet set over medium-high heat, heat the oil and add the panchphoran, letting it sizzle for a few seconds. Add the gingerroot, chilies, and garlic, and stir for a few more seconds. Add the tomatoes, salt, and sugar, stir and reduce the heat to medium; cook for about 10 minutes. Add the apricots and jalapeño peppers. Increase the heat to high and cook 5 to 7 minutes more until the mixture thickens. Remove from the heat and allow to cool, then refrigerate.

(The chutney should be made at least 2 days ahead and refrigerated so that it will thicken. Bring to room temperature before serving with the Minced-Turkey Morsels.)

Minted Melon Balls

Serves 24

It's always nice to offer some kind of fruit on an appetizer spread. These melon balls are cool, refreshing, and fragrant.

2 large honeydew melons

3 large cantaloupes

¾ cup whole mint leaves

2 tablespoons melon liqueur or crème de menthe

Cut the melons in half and remove the seeds. Scoop out the flesh using a melon baller, and put the balls in a large bowl. Mix with the mint leaves and liqueur.

Cover and refrigerate for at least 2 hours. Serve on a platter or in a shallow bowl, garnished with some additional mint, or decorate with some large leaves. If you like, serve this out of the melon shells.

Minted Melon Balls

Minced-Turkey Morsels with Tomato Chutney

The Dinner Party

Time to Serve: Between 7:00 and 9:00 P.M.

Dinner parties can be open to all sorts of inter-pretations: They can be quite intimate or very grand, casual or formal, family-style or multi-course. The type of dinner party you decide to give should depend on your preference rather than the number of guests you plan to invite. A formal dinner for six can require just as much planning as a buffet for eighteen; if you have a lot of people you

Mashed-Potato-and-Ricotta
Wontons

Savory Madeleines

"owe" invitations to, perhaps you should consider a more casual affair. Save pulling out all the stops for a smaller celebration.

The ideal number of guests for a sit-down dinner party—the number that most of us feel comfortable with—is six to ten, which also allows for an easy flow of conversation.

If you're organized, you can almost guarantee that you will have as good a time as your guests. Plan a menu that isn't wildly labor-intensive, and that doesn't require last-minute preparation and assembly. Do as much as you can—set the table, create or order your centerpieces, organize your serving pieces, order beverages, prepare dishes that don't require on-the-spot attention—ahead of time.

We've created three dinner menus here. The cool supper, perfect for summer evenings, can be made entirely beforehand, with only last-minute assembly required. The hot dinner, a heartier meal suited to colder weather, is a little more labor-intensive, but the extra work is well worth the special meal you will serve to appreciative guests. The third menu is a dinner buffet, with strong Latin overtones—the piquant, slightly sweet salsa, saffron-scented paella, and Mediterranean-style grilled vegetables. A white or red sangria will complement the Tortilla Stacks beautifully, and you may also want to offer some iced imported beers as well. The buffet here will satisfy a number of tastes, and there are plenty of alternatives for vegetarians. This is a favorite menu; the combination of colors, textures, and tastes is terrific.

Buffets can be an especially fun way to entertain, since they allow for a lot of movement and mixing among the guests, and they lend themselves to eclectic and creative dishes. Since most guests at a buffet like to try a little of this and a little of that—or even a little of everything—be sure to offer an intriguing, varied range of tastes and textures.

If your guests will stand while eating, balancing plates and glasses, plan a buffet menu that requires only a fork with which to eat the various dishes. Of course, if your guests will be seated at a table after they've loaded their plates, then a full setup, including napkin, silver, and glassware, should be placed at each seat.

If you plan to serve dinner at eight but have your guests arrive at seven-thirty, you'll probably want to serve hors d'oeuvres or snacks with before-dinner drinks. While appetizers are meant to tantalize the taste buds, they often have the opposite effect. If you serve too much, you run the risk of filling up your guests before they sit down to dinner. I've found that serving nuts, oven-roasted just before the guests arrive, along with savory marinated olives allows for predinner nibbling yet leaves appetites intact. On the other hand, if you are planning a fairly light dinner—say, soup, salad, and dessert—then serving two or three different types of heartier hors d'oeuvres would be appropriate.

Include some wonderful fresh breads from your favorite bakery (unless you are feeling ambitious and are one of those blessed people who love to bake homemade bread). Serve just one type of bread or an assortment—whatever you feel like doing.

Have a good time selecting the wines to complement these menus. I don't believe in right or wrong as far as wines and food are concerned; it's a matter of which wines you enjoy. The old rule of thumb—white wine with fish and poultry, red with meat and game—no longer applies in a world of light, fruity reds and full-bodied, rich whites. And if you're on a budget, terrific wines from Chile, Australia, Europe, and California are affordable. If you don't know wines, find a wine shop or liquor store with knowledgeable personnel, and they will be able to assist you in your selections.

HORS D'OEUVRES

Mashed-Potato-and-Ricotta Wontons

Savory Madeleines

FIRST COURSE

Baby-Lettuce Salad with Goat Cheese,
Golden Caviar, and Chives

MAIN COURSE

Poached Salmon with Plum Salsa

Lemon Dilled Rice

Asparagus Vinaigrette

Roasted Peppers and Eggplant

DESSERT

Very Berry Summer Pudding

Baby-Lettuce Salad with Goat Cheese, Golden Caviar, and Chives

Poached Salmon with Plum Salsa with Lemon Dilled Rice, Asparagus Vinaigrette, and Roasted Peppers and Eggplant

Very Berry Summer Pudding

Mashed-Potato-and-Ricotta Wontons

Makes 25 Wontons

Practically everyone loves wontons, and these totally vegetarian ones are perfect as the prelude to a dinner party—or as one of the hors d'oeuvres at a cocktail party.

1 large russet potato, baked
½ cup whole-milk ricotta
1 egg yolk
1 teaspoon chopped garlic
2 tablespoons buttermilk
½ teaspoon salt
½ teaspoon ground white pepper
1 tablespoon chopped scallion (green part only)
1 tablespoon water
1 egg white
25 wonton skins (½ package), preferably spinach or beet flavored
Vegetable oil

Scoop the potato from its skin and put it into the bowl of a food processor fitted with the metal blade; process for a few seconds. Add the ricotta, egg yolk, garlic, buttermilk, salt, pepper, and scallion, and process until the mixture is smooth; set aside and cool to room temperature.

Mix the water and the egg white in a small bowl, and brush it on the edges of the wonton skins. Put 1 teaspoon of the potato mixture in the center of each wonton skin, fold it diagonally into a triangle, and crimp the edges with a fork to seal.

In a wok or a deep skillet, heat the oil, about 2½ to 3 inches deep, over medium-high heat and deep-fry the filled wontons until they begin to turn golden and look crisp, about 3 to 5 minutes. Drain on paper towels. Transfer to a serving platter or tray and serve at once.

(These are best when served immediately, but you can fry them up to 2 hours before and crisp them in a 350° F oven for about 10 minutes before serving. You can also freeze them, uncooked, and fry them just before serving. If you freeze them, put a sheet of wax or parchment paper between each layer.)

Savory Madeleines

Makes 40 madeleines

Traditional madeleines are a sweet dessert cookie, but you'll love this savory version, redolent of Parmesan.

2 small green zucchini (about ¾ pound), shredded
1 teaspoon salt
3 tablespoons extra-virgin olive oil
½ medium yellow onion, chopped
1 teaspoon minced garlic
1 tablespoon chopped fresh basil
3 large eggs
1 tablespoon milk
⅛ teaspoon freshly ground black pepper
½ cup unbleached flour
½ tablespoon baking powder
½ cup freshly grated Parmesan cheese

Preheat the oven to 350° F. Spray 3-inch-size madeleine molds with vegetable-oil cooking spray and set aside.

In a medium bowl, mix the shredded zucchini with the salt, transfer to a colander, and let drain for 30 minutes. Rinse the zucchini under cold water, then squeeze well.

In a large nonstick skillet set over medium heat, heat the oil. Add the onion and sauté until soft, about 5 minutes. Add the garlic and stir briefly. Remove from the heat, stir in the zucchini and the basil, and set aside.

In a medium bowl, beat the eggs with the milk and the pepper, then stir in the zucchini mixture. Stir the baking powder into the flour, and add the flour mixture to the zucchini mixture; then add the Parmesan and mix well.

Place one teaspoon of batter into each madeleine mold, to fill just below the top. Bake for 10 to 15 minutes, or until puffed and golden brown. Unmold and serve immediately.

(These can be baked up to 2 hours ahead and reheated for 5 to 10 minutes in a 350° F oven, until warm.)

Baby-Lettuce Salad with Goat Cheese, Golden Caviar, and Chives

Serves 10

This first-course salad is beautiful and easy to make, and your guests will love it. Cutting the goat cheese in to shapes and decorating them with the caviar and chive arrow is a special touch—you can tie the shape into the theme of your party, if you've chosen one. Use your imagination and choose a star, a crescent, or an initial.

¾ cup walnut oil
¼ cup champagne vinegar
Salt
Freshly ground black pepper
14 ounces mild goat cheese
4 tablespoons (½ stick) unsalted butter, softened
¾ cup toasted walnuts
2 pounds mixed greens (Bibb, Oak Leaf, frisée, arugula, and watercress work well)
¼ pound golden caviar
1 bunch chives, cut into 4-inch lengths

In a small bowl, blend the oil and the vinegar; then add salt and pepper to taste. Cover and refrigerate until ready to use.

In the bowl of a food processor fitted with the metal blade, process the goat cheese and the butter until blended. Cover a board with parchment paper and coat with vegetable-oil cooking spray. Spread the cheese mixture in a layer ¾ inch thick on the board, cover with plastic wrap, and refrigerate for 2 to 4 hours, or overnight. Dip a cookie cutter into hot water and cut the goat-cheese mixture into shapes, or use the tip of a small, sharp knife. Refrigerate the cutouts until ready to use.

Toast the walnuts in a 350° F oven for 10 minutes.

Wash and dry the greens and place them in a large mixing bowl. Toss with the dressing. Put some lettuce on each salad plate and garnish with the cheese shapes, caviar, walnuts, and chives.

(You can make the goat-cheese cutouts and the dressing the day before and refrigerate. Wash and dry the greens up to a day before and store in a plastic bag. Add some paper towels to the plastic bag to prevent the greens from becoming soggy.)

Poached Salmon with Plum Salsa

Serves 10

Poach the salmon fillets in the same white wine you plan to serve. Let your budget guide your wine selection.

6 cups dry white wine
2 cups water
4 bay leaves
1 stalk celery, quartered
2 sprigs dill
1 small yellow onion, halved
10 peppercorns, bruised
1 teaspoon salt
1 sprig thyme
10 8-ounce salmon fillets
Plum Salsa (recipe follows)

In a large stockpot set over medium-high heat, combine the wine, water, bay leaves, celery, dill, onion, peppercorns, salt, and thyme. Bring to a boil and cook, uncovered, for 25 minutes. Strain the liquid into another large pot. To do this, line a strainer with a double layer of cheesecloth and place over the pot. Return the stock to the pot, and bring it back to a boil. Reduce the heat to medium-low. Place the fish in the stock, cover, and simmer for about 15 minutes, taking care that the liquid does not boil. Gently remove the salmon to a platter with a slotted spoon or spatula, cover with cheesecloth, and allow to cool to room temperature.

(The salmon can be prepared the day before and refrigerated, wrapped in plastic wrap. Bring the salmon to room temperature before serving.)

Plum Salsa

Makes about 2 cups

1 pound Santa Rosa plums, pitted and chopped
1 small red onion, chopped
1 small jalapeño pepper (or to taste), seeded and
 finely chopped
½ cup chopped cilantro
2 tablespoons fresh lemon juice
1 teaspoon sugar
Salt

In a medium bowl, combine the plums, onion, and jalapeño pepper. Stir in the cilantro, lemon juice, and sugar, and add salt to taste. Cover and refrigerate if not serving immediately.

(This can be made the day before—in fact, it's better to make it ahead of time, so that the flavors have time to blend.)

Lemon Dilled Rice

Serves 10

This rice gets its intense hue from the saffron and its rich taste from cooking in chicken stock.

7 cups chicken stock
Grated zest of 1 lemon
3 sprigs dill
1½ teaspoons salt
4 tablespoons (½ stick) unsalted butter
3 cups white rice (uncooked)
¼ cup fresh lemon juice
½ teaspoon saffron
½ cup chopped fresh dill

In a large saucepan set over medium-high heat, combine the chicken stock, lemon zest, dill sprigs, and salt, and bring to a boil. In another large saucepan, melt the butter. Add the rice and stir for 3 minutes. Pour the boiling chicken stock over the rice, bring back to a boil, reduce heat to medium, cover, and cook for 20 to 25 minutes, or until the rice is soft and most of the liquid is absorbed. Remove from the heat and stir in the lemon juice, saffron, and chopped dill. Transfer to a bowl and refrigerate until ready to serve.

(This can be made the day before.)

Asparagus Vinaigrette

Serves 10

3 pounds pencil-thin asparagus, washed and
 trimmed
1 cup extra-virgin olive oil
½ cup red-wine vinegar
½ cup chopped fresh herbs (mint, dill, and basil
 work well)
1 teaspoon salt
½ teaspoon freshly ground black pepper

Bring a large pot of water to a boil. Place the asparagus in the boiling water and cook for 2 minutes. Remove the asparagus, plunge them into ice water, drain, and set aside.

In a medium bowl, mix the olive oil, vinegar, herbs, salt, and pepper. Add the asparagus, mix to coat with the vinaigrette, and let marinate for about 30 minutes. Remove from the marinade before refrigerating.

(This dish can be made up to a day before and refrigerated.)

Roasted Peppers and Eggplant

Serves 10

5 large red bell peppers
10 Japanese eggplant
¼ cup extra-virgin olive oil
1 teaspoon fresh lemon juice
1 garlic clove, minced
½ teaspoon salt
½ teaspoon freshly ground black pepper
½ cup chopped fresh herbs (rosemary and thyme work well)

Cut the peppers in half lengthwise, then cut each half, lengthwise, into 4 rectangular pieces. Remove the seeds. Cut the eggplant in half lengthwise.

In a large bowl, mix the olive oil, lemon juice, garlic, salt, pepper, and herbs. Add the peppers and the eggplant, and toss with your hands until the vegetables are well coated. Let them stand at room temperature for about 2 hours.

Preheat the oven to 400° F. Remove the vegetables from the marinade and place them on a baking sheet in a single layer. Bake for 20 to 25 minutes, or until the vegetables are soft but still hold their shape. They may also be grilled, indoors or out. Remove from the oven and let cool to room temperature before serving.

(This can be made earlier in the day and kept at room temperature.)

Very Berry Summer Pudding

Serves 10

This is beautiful, impressive, and easy to make. Use the best-quality bread you can find.

28 slices day-old, thinly sliced white bread
8 cups raspberries (or a combination of raspberries, strawberries, and blackberries), fresh or frozen
1 cup sugar
¼ cup crème de cassis
1 pint fresh raspberries
1 bunch mint leaves

Remove the crusts from the bread. Cover the bottom of a 2-quart bowl with a slice of bread. Arrange additional slices, slightly overlapping, around the inside of the bowl, until you reach the top. You will have bread left over.

In a large pot set over medium heat, combine the berries, sugar, and cassis. Simmer, stirring occasionally, until the sugar has dissolved and the berries are slightly crushed. Remove from the heat and let cool for 25 to 30 minutes.

Put half the berry mixture into the mold and cover with a few more slices of bread. Repeat with the rest of the berries, and finish with a layer of bread. Cover with a round of wax paper that has been cut to fit the inside of the mold. Place a plate on top of the wax paper in the mold, then place a 3-pound weight on the plate. Refrigerate overnight, or up to 2 days. When ready to serve, remove the weight, plate, and wax paper, and invert the pudding onto a serving plate. Garnish with raspberries and mint leaves.

HORS D'OEUVRES

Savory Madeleines

(see page 129)

FIRST COURSE

Borscht

MAIN COURSE

Chicken Breasts Stuffed with Ricotta Pesto

Stuffed Potato Boxes

Nutmeg-Carrot Purée

Yellow and Green Beans

DESSERT

Mocha-Fudge Torte

Borscht

Serves 10

Soups as first courses are nothing new, though lately they seem to have been replaced with salad or pasta starters. The color and savory taste of this borscht are very satisfying; it is well worth the effort it takes to make.

12 cups Chicken Stock (recipe follows)
4 large beets
1 large potato (about ¾ pound)
1 medium green cabbage
1 cooked carrot, shredded (from Chicken Stock)
½ cup plus 2 tablespoons ketchup
1 tablespoon sugar
1 tablespoon fresh lemon juice
1½ cups sour cream
Fresh dill

First, prepare the Chicken Stock.

Wash the beets; place in a plastic bag and microwave at full power for 10 to 15 minutes, or until soft but not mushy. Rinse them under cold water, and peel. Coarsely shred them into a bowl, and set aside.

Peel the potato and cut it into 1- to 1½-inch chunks. Remove the core and the outer leaves from the cabbage and quarter it. Cut each quarter into ½-inch-thick slices.

Bring the Chicken Stock to a simmer. Add the potato and cook for about 5 minutes. Add the cabbage, shredded carrot, and shredded beets, and simmer for 15 minutes more until the vegetables are cooked. Stir in the ketchup, sugar, and lemon juice. Bring to a boil, then reduce the heat and simmer until ready to serve.

Ladle the hot soup into bowls and garnish with a tablespoonful or more of sour cream and some fresh dill.

(This borscht is best made a day ahead. Refrigerate it after cooking, and reheat before serving—this borscht is not good cold.)

Chicken Stock

Makes about 12 cups

1 chicken carcass, with some meat
3 quarts water
1 medium onion, peeled and quartered
1 large carrot, peeled
1 medium parsnip
1 celery stalk, halved
1 tablespoon salt
1 teaspoon dried basil

In a large stockpot set over high heat, bring the chicken bones, water, onion, carrot, parsnip, celery, salt, and basil to a boil. Reduce the heat to low and simmer for 30 minutes. Strain the mixture, and discard all the solids *except* the carrot. Put the stock back into the pot and set aside. Coarsely shred the carrot and set aside.

Chicken Breasts Stuffed with Ricotta Pesto

Serves 10

This pale green stuffing against the white chicken and golden skin makes a stunning presentation.

1 teaspoon minced garlic
1 cup firmly packed basil leaves
2 cups whole-milk ricotta
3 tablespoons freshly grated Parmesan cheese
1½ teaspoons salt
1½ teaspoons freshly ground black pepper
5 large whole chicken breasts, boned but not
  split, skin on, lightly pounded
10 large fresh basil leaves

In a food processor fitted with the metal blade, combine the garlic, basil, ricotta, Parmesan, 1 teaspoon of the salt, and 1 teaspoon of the pepper. Process until well blended, about 1 minute, adjust the seasonings, and set aside.

Carefully remove the skins from the chicken breasts and reserve them. Lay the chicken breasts flat and sprinkle them with the remaining salt and pepper. Place 2 basil leaves on each breast. Divide the cheese mixture equally among the chicken breasts and spread into an even coat.

Preheat the oven to 350° F, or prepare a charcoal grill and let the coals come to a gray ash.

Roll the breasts from the widest part of the pointed end. Place each roll on a piece of chicken skin and wrap the skin around the roll, like an envelope. With kitchen string, tie each roll once lengthwise and across three or four times. Grill or bake in an 11 × 14-inch baking dish for 25 to 30 minutes, or until the chicken looks golden brown, feels firm to the touch, and the juices run clear.

Remove the string before serving, and cut the chicken rolls into 7 to 10 slices at an angle.

(Stuff the chicken breasts the day before and refrigerate. Take them out of the refrigerator ½ hour before cooking.)

Stuffed Potato Boxes

Serves 10

The woodsy flavor of the mushrooms and the sweet taste of cooked onions enriched with cream make this a particularly delectable dish. However, your guests will happily suspend any thoughts of diets when enjoying these potatoes. If your budget allows, use a combination of exotic and domestic mushrooms.

10 large russet potatoes (about 3/4 pound each)
½ cup extra-virgin olive oil
1 large yellow onion, thinly sliced
1 teaspoon minced garlic
1½ pounds trimmed mushrooms
1 tablespoon chopped fresh basil
¾ cup heavy cream
Salt
Freshly ground pepper

Peel the potatoes and trim them into a box shape. Leaving a shell about ½ inch thick on all four sides and at the bottom, cut out a rectangle within the box. Working carefully inside the cut marks, scoop out the potato with a teaspoon. Keep the potato shells in cold water and set aside. Discard the scooped-out potato.

Preheat the oven to 350° F.

In a large nonstick skillet set over medium heat, heat 2 tablespoons of the olive oil. Add the onion and garlic and sauté until the onion is golden, about 10 minutes. Remove the onion and garlic from the skillet and set aside. Add 2 more tablespoons of the olive oil to the skillet and sauté the mushrooms until golden brown, about 10 minutes. Return the onions and garlic to the skillet, add the basil, and cook 5 minutes more. Remove from the heat.

In a small saucepan set over medium heat, heat the cream until it begins to thicken. Add it to the mushroom-onion mixture, then season with salt and pepper to taste. Remove from the heat and set aside until you are ready to fill the potato boxes.

Dry the potatoes and brush them with olive oil. Bake them on a cookie sheet for 30 to 40 minutes, or until golden brown. Warm the filling and spoon some into each potato. Serve at once.

(The potatoes can be hollowed out and placed in water the day before the party. They can be cooked early the next day, and filled and warmed before serving. The mushroom-onion filling can be made up to 2 days ahead and refrigerated.)

Borscht

Chicken Breasts Stuffed
with Ricotta Pesto
Stuffed Potato Boxes
Nutmeg-Carrot Purée

Mocha-Fudge Torte

Nutmeg-Carrot Purée

Serves 10

These carrots taste like yams. The addition of the freshly grated nutmeg adds a kick, and cooking the carrots in broth instead of water adds another dimension to the flavor.

2 quarts chicken stock
10 jumbo carrots
¼ pound (1 stick) unsalted butter, softened
1 teaspoon salt
2 teaspoons freshly grated nutmeg

In a large saucepan set over high heat, bring the stock to a boil. Peel the carrots and cut into 2-inch pieces. Add the carrots to the boiling stock and cook 15 to 20 minutes, or until soft. Drain, then transfer the carrots to the bowl of a food processor fitted with the metal blade. Process until smooth, about 3 to 5 minutes, then add the butter, salt, and nutmeg, and process a minute more.

(This can be prepared the day before and refrigerated; warm the purée before serving. To reheat, bring the purée to room temperature. Cover and heat in a 350° F oven for 30 minutes.)

Yellow and Green Beans

Serves 10

If yellow wax beans are unavailable, you can use green beans alone. However, the pale-yellow beans look very dramatic against the green.

1 pound yellow wax beans
1 pound green beans
2 tablespoons (¼ stick) unsalted butter
Salt
Freshly ground black pepper

Wash and trim the beans. In a large saucepan put enough water to cover the beans, and bring to a boil over high heat. Add the beans and cook for about 3 minutes, or until crisp-tender. Plunge them into ice water, then drain in a colander.

Just before serving melt the butter in a large non-stick skillet set over medium heat. Add the beans and cook until just warmed through. Add salt and pepper to taste and serve at once.

(Boil the beans the morning of your party and refrigerate until ready to finish.)

Mocha-Fudge Torte

Serves 10

This is a very rich flourless chocolate dessert. You can add a dollop of whipped cream, but it really isn't needed.

8 ounces semisweet chocolate, broken into bits, or chocolate chips
½ pound (2 sticks) unsalted butter, softened
½ cup very strong coffee
1 cup granulated sugar
4 large eggs, at room temperature
Confectioners' sugar
Candied violets

Preheat the oven to 350° F. Line the bottom of a 9-inch springform cake pan with parchment paper and coat with vegetable-oil cooking spray. Set aside.

In a medium saucepan set over low heat, combine the chocolate, butter, coffee, and granulated sugar. Cook, stirring constantly, until the chocolate is melted. Remove from the heat and let cool slightly.

In the bowl of an electric mixer, beat the eggs until they are pale yellow, about 2 minutes, then add the chocolate mixture and blend well. Pour the batter into the prepared pan. Bake for 30 to 35 minutes, or until the top cracks. Cool, cover with foil, and refrigerate at least overnight.

When ready to serve, remove from the springform but leave on base; sift confectioners' sugar over the top of the cake, and decorate with candied violets.

(This torte can be made up to 2 weeks ahead and frozen. Thaw at room temperature for about 1½ hours before serving.)

Tortilla Stack with Papaya Salsa

Paella

Herb-Marinated Grilled Vegetables

Blood-Orange-and-Roasted-Beet Salad over Greens

White Beans with Roasted Shallots and Thyme

Burgundy Baked Bosc Pears

Orange-Chocolate-Chunk Bundt Cake

Black-and-Whites

Tortilla Stack with Papaya Salsa

Makes 32 to 40 wedges

A different take on an old standby. These quesadillas are stacked instead of folded, baked instead of fried. If you prefer, substitute your favorite salsa for the papaya. Try to find handmade tortillas—they make a difference.

12 7-inch flour tortillas
4 tablespoons (½ stick) unsalted butter, melted
¾ cup freshly grated Parmesan cheese
4 cups shredded mozzarella or Jack cheese, or a combination of the two
Papaya Salsa (recipe follows)

Preheat the oven to 375° F. Coat a baking sheet with vegetable-oil cooking spray and set aside.

Brush a tortilla with melted butter. Sprinkle with ½ teaspoon of the Parmesan, then with about ¼ cup of the shredded cheese, then with 1 tablespoon of the Papaya Salsa. Top with a second tortilla, and repeat the butter, cheeses, and salsa layers, and top with a third tortilla to make one stack. Make three more stacks with the remaining tortillas, butter, cheeses, and salsa, so that you have four stacks of three tortillas each. Brush the top of each stack with melted butter and sprinkle with Parmesan.

Place the stacks on the baking sheet and bake for 10 to 15 minutes, or until the tops begin to turn golden brown and the cheese is melted. Remove from the oven and let stand a minute before cutting into 8 to 10 wedges. Transfer to a serving platter and serve at once.

(You can assemble these up to 2 days ahead. Cover and refrigerate.)

Papaya Salsa

Makes about 1½ cups

1 large papaya, peeled, seeded, and chopped
½ cup red onion, chopped
1 bunch cilantro, chopped
½ jalapeño pepper, seeded and minced (more if
   you like it hot!)
½ teaspoon salt
1 tablespoon fresh lemon juice

In a small bowl, combine the papaya, onion, cilantro, jalapeño pepper, salt, and lemon juice. Cover and refrigerate for at least 1 hour to allow the flavors to marry.

Paella

Serves 20

Don't let the lengthy instructions intimidate you—this version of paella is well worth the effort. The sauce is made beforehand, and the other ingredients are all cooked separately, so that they maintain their individual taste. You can use other firm-fleshed fish, or add more shellfish if you prefer. This dish is wonderful the next day, too, so you might want to make a little extra.

Tomato Sauce

Makes about 4 quarts

¼ cup extra-virgin olive oil
3 medium yellow onions, thinly sliced
8 large garlic cloves, minced
3 cups chopped green, yellow, and red peppers
   (about 1 of each pepper)
3 28-ounce cans whole tomatoes
2 tablespoons dried basil
1 tablespoon dried oregano
1 teaspoon cayenne pepper, or to taste
1½ tablespoons salt

2 tablespoons paprika
¼ cup fresh lemon juice
1 cup white wine
½ cup ketchup

In a 4- to 6-quart stainless or enameled saucepan set over medium heat, heat the oil. Add the onion and cook until soft and golden. Add the minced garlic and stir for a few seconds. Add the chopped peppers and cook for a few minutes.

Meanwhile, drain the tomatoes, reserving the juice, cut each tomato into 3 pieces. Add to the saucepan along with the tomato juice, and bring to a boil. Stir in the basil, oregano, cayenne, salt, and paprika, and cook for about 30 minutes. Adjust the seasonings, then add the lemon juice, wine, and ketchup, and cook for about 10 minutes more. Set aside until ready to use.

This sauce can be made up to 3 days ahead. Finish making the paella on the day of your party with:

3 medium chicken breasts, skinned, boned, split,
   and cut into 1-inch cubes
1½ teaspoons salt
¼ cup extra-virgin olive oil
2 pounds shark, cut into 1-inch cubes
10 sweet Italian sausages
2 pounds large (sea) scallops
2 pounds New Zealand green tip mussels, or
   black mussels
2 pounds shrimp (21 to 25 per pound with shells
   on), peeled and deveined

4 cups white rice (uncooked)
2 quarts chicken stock
1 teaspoon saffron

1 bunch cilantro, chopped, as garnish

Place the chicken breast pieces in a bowl. Toss with ½ teaspoon of the salt and 1 tablespoon of the olive oil. Transfer to a medium nonstick skillet set over medium heat and cook until the chicken is opaque but not browned, about 5 minutes. Remove from the heat. Place the chicken in a bowl and set aside.

In another bowl, toss the shark cubes with ½ teaspoon of the salt and 1 tablespoon of the olive oil. Transfer to a medium nonstick skillet set over high heat and

Tortilla Stack
with Papaya Salsa

Paella

White Beans with
Roasted Shallots
and Thyme

Herb-Marinated Grilled Vegetables

Blood-Orange-and-
Roasted-Beet Salad
over Greens

cook until opaque, about 5 minutes. Remove from the heat. Place the shark in a bowl and set aside.

In a large nonstick skillet set over medium-high heat, cook the sausages for 10 to 15 minutes until cooked through, turning occasionally. Cut each sausage into 4 or 5 pieces. Place the sausage in a bowl and set aside.

In another bowl, toss the scallops with ½ teaspoon of the salt and 1 tablespoon of the olive oil. Transfer to a medium nonstick skillet set over high heat and cook until the scallops are slightly browned on each side, about 5 or 6 minutes.

To cook the mussels, bring a large pot of water to a boil. Put in the mussels and cover. Cook until the shells open, 5 to 7 minutes. Drain, and remove the mussels from their shells, at the same time removing any dirt or grit. Clean the mussels under cold running water and set aside. Reserve about 24 of the shell halves.

To cook the shrimp, bring a large pot of water to a boil. Add the shrimp and simmer until they just turn pink, about 3 minutes. Drain and place the shrimp in ice water for a few minutes. Drain, place the shrimp in a bowl, and set aside.

To prepare the rice, bring the chicken stock to a boil in a large saucepan. In a large nonstick skillet set over high heat, heat the remaining 1 tablespoon of oil. Add the rice and stir until the grains are coated. Add the rice to the chicken stock, stir in the saffron, and bring to a boil. Reduce the heat to low, cover, and cook for about 20 minutes, or until the rice is fluffy and all the stock is absorbed.

To assemble the paella, mix half the Tomato Sauce with the chicken, shark, scallops, sausage, mussels, and shrimp in a large bowl. Mix the other half with the rice. Combine the two mixtures and place in large pot. Warm over medium-low heat.

When ready to serve, transfer the paella to a large serving platter and sprinkle with the chopped cilantro. Pick out some of the mussels and place them in the reserved shells. Decorate the platter with the mussels in their shells.

Herb-Marinated Grilled Vegetables

Serves 20

These vegetables can be grilled earlier in the day and served at room temperature. They hold up very well, but be careful with substitutions: broccoli, cauliflower, or greens will not yield the same results.

3 tablespoons minced garlic
¼ cup fresh rosemary leaves
1 teaspoon freshly ground black pepper
2 teaspoons salt
¾ cup extra-virgin olive oil
1¼ cups red- or white-wine vinegar
10 bay leaves

2 pounds green bell peppers
2 pounds red bell peppers
2 pounds yellow bell peppers
3 pounds zucchini
3 pounds yellow squash
2 pounds asparagus
½ cup chopped fresh herbs (basil, cilantro, mint, or a combination)

In a medium bowl, combine the garlic, rosemary, pepper, salt, olive oil, vinegar, and bay leaves. Set aside for about 2 hours at room temperature to allow the flavors to meld.

Halve all the peppers lengthwise and clean them. Cut the ends off the zucchini and the yellow squash and cut in half lengthwise. Trim the asparagus.

Marinate the vegetables separately: the three types of peppers in one bowl, the two types of squash in another, the asparagus in another. Cover with plastic wrap and refrigerate for up to 2 days, turning a couple of times.

Prepare a charcoal grill until the coals are white and there are no flames. Grill the peppers until they are marked and soft. Remove from the fire and set aside. Repeat with the squash, and then with the asparagus.

Cut the peppers in half again and quarter the squash; leave the asparagus whole. Place on a serving platter and set aside.

When ready to serve, sprinkle the fresh herbs on top of the vegetables.

(Marinate the vegetables for up to 2 days, and grill them the day of your party. They're wonderful served at room temperature.)

Blood-Orange-and-Roasted-Beet Salad over Greens

Serves 20

The colors in this dish are extraordinary. Although the combination is exotic, the ingredients work extremely well together. Blood oranges are preferable because of their unusual color and tart taste. Baking will cause the beets to retain their intense hue.

½ cup extra-virgin olive oil
¼ cup balsamic vinegar
1½ teaspoons salt
½ teaspoon freshly ground black pepper
10 large beets, with greens
2 bunches spinach
8 blood oranges

First, make the dressing: Mix the oil, vinegar, salt, and pepper in a small bowl. Adjust the seasonings and set aside.

Preheat the oven to 450° F.

Scrub but do not peel the beets; remove and reserve the greens. Wrap each beet in aluminum foil and bake for 1 to 1½ hours, or until a toothpick pierces to the center. Unwrap the beets and hold under cold running water so their skins slip off. Slice the beets about ¼ inch thick and set aside.

Bring a large pot of water to a boil. Clean and stem the spinach and the beet greens. Blanch the greens until just wilted but still bright green, about 4 to 5 minutes.

Drain well and let cool. Transfer the greens to a large bowl and mix with ¼ cup of the dressing.

Peel the oranges and slice them about ¼-inch thick. Mix the sliced beets and oranges in a large bowl. Toss gently with the remaining dressing.

Place the greens on a platter, and arrange the beets and oranges on top of them.

(Prepare everything the morning of the party and refrigerate. Bring to room temperature and assemble just before serving.)

White Beans with Roasted Shallots and Thyme

Serves 20

Although the bacon or pancetta adds a wonderful rich flavor, this becomes a vegetarian dish by omitting it. Add a little more thyme and garlic, and adjust the salt and pepper at the end.

2 pounds small uncooked white beans (cannellini or great northern beans work well)
2 or 3 thick slices bacon or pancetta
2 tablespoons chopped garlic
Salt
1 bunch fresh thyme
½ cup extra-virgin olive oil
1½ pounds shallots
Freshly ground black pepper

Rinse and pick over the beans in a colander under cold running water. Place them in a large bowl, cover with cold water, and let stand overnight. Drain. Transfer the beans to a large saucepan, add cold water to about 2 inches higher than the beans, and add the bacon or pancetta and the garlic. Bring to a boil over high heat, add salt to taste and a few branches of the thyme, then reduce the heat to low. Cover and let simmer for 30 to 40 minutes, or until the beans are tender. Drain and toss the beans with ¼ cup of the olive oil.

Preheat the oven to 350° F.

While the beans cook, peel the shallots. Place them in a large bowl and toss with the remaining ¼ cup of olive oil and a few branches of the thyme. Place the shallots on a baking sheet and bake for 30 to 40 minutes or until they are soft and golden brown. Remove from the oven.

Combine the beans and the shallots, and transfer the mixture to an ovenproof baking dish. Bake, uncovered, for 15 minutes. Remove from the oven and add salt and pepper to taste. Serve on a platter garnished with the remaining fresh thyme.

(This can be made the morning of your party and covered but not refrigerated. Serve at room temperature.)

Burgundy Baked Bosc Pears

Serves 20

Everyone will ask you for this recipe. The pears look lacquered and are almost too beautiful to eat. Leave a couple of the pears whole to garnish the serving plate.

12 Bosc pears, unpeeled, stems intact
1½ cups or more red Burgundy wine
1 cup sugar

Preheat the oven to 375° F.

Slice off the bottoms of the pears. Place the pears upright in a shallow baking dish. Pour the wine over the pears, then sprinkle them with ½ cup of the sugar.

Bake the pears for 35 to 45 minutes, basting every 10 minutes with the pan juices, and adding a little more wine if too much evaporates. Sprinkle the remaining ½ cup of sugar over the pears and bake for about 20 minutes more, or until they are tender when pierced and look lacquered. Remove from the oven and let cool in the baking dish; do not refrigerate. Just before serving, cut 10 of the pears in halves or quarters and arrange on a platter, garnishing with two whole pears.

(Make these the morning of your party, and don't refrigerate.)

Orange-Chocolate-Chunk Bundt Cake

Makes one 10-inch bundt cake

The combination of orange and chocolate is wonderful in this rich, dense cake. This recipe is adapted from *The Loaves and Fishes Party Cookbook*, by Anna Pump and Sybille Pump.

1 cup (2 sticks) unsalted butter, softened
2⅔ cups sugar
6 large eggs
Grated zest of one medium orange
1 teaspoon baking powder
1 cup sour cream
1 teaspoon orange liqueur, such as Grand Marnier or Cointreau
3 cups unbleached flour
8 ounces semisweet chocolate, broken into small chunks
1¼ cups Citrus Glaze (recipe follows)

Preheat the oven to 350° F. Butter a 10-inch Teflon-coated bundt pan and set aside. (If you're not using a Teflon bundt pan, spray with vegetable-oil spray.)

In the bowl of an electric mixer, combine the butter and sugar. Cream at medium speed until light yellow and fluffy, about 3 minutes. Beat the eggs in one at a time, then beat in the orange zest, baking powder, sour cream, orange liqueur, and 2 cups of the flour. When the mixture is well blended, add the remaining flour and the chocolate chunks, and mix well.

Pour the batter into the prepared pan. Bake for 1 hour, or until a cake tester comes out clean. Remove from the oven and let cool for 10 minutes.

With the cake still in the pan, pour the Citrus Glaze over the cake and let set for 20 minutes. Unmold onto a cake stand or platter.

(Make this cake at least 1 day in advance; it freezes beautifully for up to 1 month. Glaze and unmold before freezing.)

Citrus Glaze

1 cup fresh orange juice
¼ cup fresh lemon juice
⅔ cup sugar
1 tablespoon orange liqueur, such as Grand
    Marnier or Cointreau

In a small saucepan set over medium heat, combine the orange juice, lemon juice, sugar, and orange liqueur. Heat until the sugar dissolves, about 5 minutes; do not boil. Set aside.

Burgundy Baked Bosc Pears

Black-and-Whites

Makes about 24 2-inch cookies

This luxurious adaptation, from *Star Desserts* by Emily Luchetti, is a super-rich take on an old classic.

1½ cups (3 sticks) cold unsalted butter
¾ cup granulated sugar
2¼ cups unbleached flour
¾ cup Dutch-process cocoa (sift first, then
    measure)
⅛ teaspoon salt

1½ cups Mascarpone cheese, or 12 ounces
    softened cream cheese
2 tablespoons granulated sugar
¼ teaspoon vanilla extract
¼ teaspoon Amaretto or almond extract
Confectioners' sugar (optional)

Line baking sheets with parchment paper and coat with vegetable-oil cooking spray.

In the bowl of an electric mixer, combine the butter and the sugar, and mix at low speed for 20 seconds. Add the flour, cocoa, and salt, and mix at low speed for 5 minutes, or until the dough comes together.

Gather the dough into a ball and place on a floured board. Roll out ¼ inch thick. Cut out the dough with a 2-inch cookie cutter; a heart or star shape is festive. Place the cookies on the prepared sheets and refrigerate the cutouts for at least 1 hour.

Preheat the oven to 250° F. Bake for about 1 hour, or until firm. Remove to a rack to cool completely before filling.

While the cookies bake, prepare the filling. In a small bowl, mix the Mascarpone, sugar, vanilla, and Amaretto. Set aside.

To make the cookies, spread about 1 teaspoon of the cheese mixture on the bottom of one cookie and cover with the bottom of another to make a sandwich. Dust with confectioners' sugar if you like.

(Bake the cookies up to a month in advance and freeze them. Fill them with the cheese mixture the day you plan to serve them.)

The Dessert Party

Time to Serve: After 9:00 P.M.

People tend to be passionate about dessert, whether their confection of choice is chocolate cake, lemon mousse, apple pie à la mode, or something else entirely. And many of us would rather watch our calories all day—or even all week—in order to indulge our sweet tooth occasionally. Even the most stoic, virtuous, and dietarily circumspect of folk will melt, as it were, throwing all caution to the winds, when a delicious *dolce* is placed in front of them.

With that in mind, the perfect event for some would entail cutting to the chase and getting down to business: a party dedicated exclusively to desserts, given after the dinner hour, from about 9:00 P.M. onward. You and your guests can really have a great time with this one. The only rule is to offer a broad selection of flavors, textures, and looks (although you could also have a theme, such as all-chocolate). Have some beautiful seasonal fruit on hand for purists (as well as for those who cannot eat sugar or have to watch their cholesterol), a nice choice of cheeses and crackers (a much-neglected and underappreciated form of dessert in America), something chocolaty, something lemony, something rich, something light. Again, thrill and surprise the palate with varieties of warm, cool, cold, crunchy, crisp, and meltingly soft.

When you plan the menu for your dessert party, keep in mind that you don't *have* to make everything from scratch. However, if you love to bake, pull out all the stops—as well as all your favorite recipes. If you'd rather let someone else do the work, then use all those food resources you've gathered over time. Pick up desserts from your favorite pastry shop, bakery, or restaurant, or put together a combination of homemade and store-bought sweets. The only sin at a dessert party is in not having enough.

The following dessert-party menu only scratches the creative surface. According to personal taste and preference, feel free to substitute any of these recipes with your favorites or with store-bought sweets.

Dessert parties also allow creativity in the choice of beverages. Offer a few different coffees—perhaps one flavored, and always one decaffeinated—and a few teas. If you're so inclined and have the equipment, caffè latte, cappuccino, and espresso add flair.

You can also offer a selection of after-dinner drinks. You don't have to pour costly Château d'Yquem these days; many delicious and inexpensive California dessert wines, such as Essencia, are available.

Another alternative is to select liqueurs that echo the flavors of the desserts—Framboise with the Very Berry Summer Pudding, Fra Angelico with a pecan tart, or Cuarenta y Tres with a smooth vanilla custard. Liqueurs and cordials are nice in coffee or served over ice. If you find them a bit too sweet on their own, cut them with a tiny splash of vodka after pouring.

Dessert Party Menu—Serves 30

Purchased Fruit Tarts, Strudels,
Custard Tarts, and Cookies

Poached Fruits in Wine

Chocolate Pâté

Orange-Chocolate-Chunk Bundt Cake (see page 144)
(Make 2 cakes.)

Very Berry Summer Pudding (see page 132)
(Make 2 puddings.)

Lemon-Walnut Squares (see page 156)
(Make 3 batches.)

Chocolate-Pepper Hearts (see page 155)
(Make 3 batches.)

Dessert Party

Orange-Chocolate-Chunk
Bundt Cake

Poached Fruits in Wine

Serves 30

This variety of fruits poached in different wines and spices, placed in clear, wide-mouth flower vases with the poaching liquid or on a cake stand, makes a beautiful addition to a dessert buffet. You can make all of the fruits suggested here, or make one and increase the recipe accordingly. These call for large amounts of wine, so look for a good buy. (It's best to serve these poached fruits separately rather than combined. Cut one or two of them in half to see the color variations. They're wonderful served in the poaching liquid, but you can serve them out of their liquids, too.)

Poached Pears in Red Wine

8 firm but ripe Bosc pears
2 750-milliliter bottles red wine (Cabernet, Pinot Noir, or a Burgundy)
Peel from one lemon
¼ cup fresh lemon juice
1½ cups sugar
1 cinnamon stick
1 vanilla bean
¼ cup pear brandy or brandy

Peel the pears, but leave the stems on.

In a large pot set over high heat, combine the wine, lemon peel, lemon juice, sugar, cinnamon, vanilla, and brandy, and boil for 5 minutes. Add the pears, reduce the heat to low, cover, and simmer for 30 minutes, or until the pears are burgundy in color. Remove from the heat and let the pears cool in the poaching liquid. Refrigerate in the liquid at least overnight or for up to 3 days.

Poached Pears in White Wine

8 firm but ripe Bartlett or Anjou pears
2 750-milliliter bottles white wine (Chardonnay, Fumé Blanc, Sauvignon Blanc)
Peel from one lemon
¼ cup fresh lemon juice
1½ cups sugar
1 tablespoon allspice berries
2 vanilla beans

Peel the pears but leave the stems on.

In a large pot, set over high heat, combine the wine, lemon peel, lemon juice, sugar, allspice, and vanilla, and boil for 5 minutes. Add the pears, reduce the heat to low, cover, and simmer for 30 minutes. Remove from the heat and let the pears cool in the poaching liquid. Refrigerate in the liquid at least overnight or for up to 3 days.

Poached Cherries in White Wine

1 750-milliliter bottle white wine (such as Riesling)
Peel from one lemon
¼ cup fresh lemon juice
½ cup sugar
10 whole cloves
1 vanilla bean
¼ cup orange liqueur, such as Grand Marnier
2 pounds firm white Rainier or Queen Anne cherries, with stems

In a medium pot set over high heat, combine the wine, lemon peel, lemon juice, sugar, cloves, vanilla, and orange liqueur and boil for 5 minutes. Add the cherries, reduce the heat to low, cover, and simmer for 10 minutes. Remove from the heat and let the cherries cool in the poaching liquid. Refrigerate in the liquid at least overnight or for up to 3 days.

(If you can't find white cherries, use Bing cherries; substitute red wine for the white and omit the orange liqueur.)

Poached Peaches in Rosé Wine

8 firm but ripe peaches
2 750-milliliter bottles rosé wine
Peel from one lemon
¼ cup fresh lemon juice
1½ cups sugar
1 cinnamon stick
1 tablespoon mixed peppercorns
¼ cup peach brandy

Bring a large pot of water to a boil. Score the bottom of the peaches, add them to the boiling water, and cook for about 2 to 3 minutes, or until the skin starts to peel. Remove and let cool slightly before peeling.

In a large pot set over high heat, combine the wine, lemon peel, lemon juice, sugar, cinnamon, peppercorns, and brandy, and boil for 5 minutes. Add the peaches, reduce the heat to low, cover, and simmer for 10 to 15 minutes. Remove from the heat and let the peaches cool in the poaching liquid. Refrigerate in the liquid at least overnight or for up to 3 days.

Chocolate Pâté

Serves 30

This dessert falls somewhere between a fruitcake and a candy bar. If you can't find dried cherries, a mixture of glacéed fruits and golden raisins works well; it's not necessary to soak them in hot water.

1 cup dried cherries
1 cup hot water
6 ounces bittersweet chocolate
¾ cup sugar
4 tablespoons water
1 cup Dutch-process cocoa (sift before
  measuring)
¾ cup (1½ sticks) unsalted butter, softened
1 large egg*
2 egg yolks*
1 cup unsalted pistachio nuts, shelled and toasted
  (toast for 10 minutes in a 350° F oven)

1 11-ounce package vanilla wafers or butter cookies, broken into ½-inch bits

Line a 6-cup (8½ × 4½ × 2½-inch) loaf pan with plastic wrap, and set aside.

Soak the dried cherries in the hot water for 30 minutes.

Meanwhile, melt the bittersweet chocolate in the top of a double boiler over high heat.

In a small saucepan set over low heat, combine the sugar and the 4 tablespoons of water, and cook until the sugar has dissolved. Turn off the heat.

In the bowl of an electric mixer, combine the cocoa and the butter and beat at medium speed for 3 minutes until smooth. Stir in the sugar syrup, then the melted chocolate. Beat the egg and the egg yolks in a small bowl. Drain the cherries. With a wooden spoon, fold in the cherries, nuts, and cookie bits so they are well incorporated.

Spoon the mixture into the loaf pan, press down, and let settle. Cover with plastic wrap and refrigerate at least overnight.

Unmold the pâté, dust with a little cocoa powder, and sprinkle with some chopped pistachio nuts.

Cut the pâté into 15 to 18 slices, then cut these in half again, as the pâté is very rich.

(You can make this up to a week ahead and refrigerate.)

Although this recipe calls for uncooked eggs, the U.S. Department of Agriculture has found them to be a potential carrier of food-borne illnesses, and recommends that diners avoid them. Egg substitutes may be used instead; check packages for substitutions.

The Late-Supper Party

Time to Serve: After 10:00 P.M.

Late-evening supper parties can be a wonderfully different way to entertain. That sense of gleeful naughtiness from staying up past one's bedtime and indulging in delicious food is so sinfully appealing. You can serve a late supper any time after 10:00 P.M., depending on how night-owlish you and your guests may be. Late suppers are perfect for after the theater and concerts.

The food at a late-night meal should be a little lighter than what you would serve at a more conventional hour; no one should feel so stuffed and uncomfortable that he or she will have trouble falling asleep. One-dish entrees work particularly well. This is the perfect time to serve lasagna, sandwiches, casseroles, hearty soups, or our suggested menu. Late suppers also provide an opportunity for a great potluck meal.

This meal should ideally be one that you can prepare earlier in the day, so that all you will have to do before serving it is to heat up whatever needs to be warmed, toss the salad (if you are serving one), and set the dishes out (the last can even be done beforehand).

Having three desserts on this menu isn't as excessive as it seems—sweet tooths seem to come out late in the evening, and none of these desserts is terribly rich or over-the-top.

Late-Supper Party Menu—Serves 8

Fresh Salmon Cakes

Couscous Salad with Vegetables and Dried Cranberries

Bitter-Greens Salad

Chocolate-Pepper Hearts

Lemon-Walnut Squares

Intoxicating Fruit

Late-Supper Party

Bitter-Greens Salad

Fresh Salmon Cakes and Couscous Salad with Vegetables and Dried Cranberries

Lemon-Walnut Squares and Chocolate-Pepper Hearts

Fresh Salmon Cakes

Makes 20 2½-inch cakes

These may remind you of salmon croquettes, but they are sautéed rather than deep-fried, and the seasonings are much zippier. A sauce isn't necessary because the taste and texture of the salmon are so luxurious.

1½ pounds salmon fillet
3 large eggs
¾ cup milk or half-and-half
5 tablespoons mayonnaise
1½ teaspoons Dijon mustard
1½ teaspoons salt
½ teaspoon freshly ground black pepper
1 tablespoon chopped fresh parsley
¼ cup chopped scallions (white and green parts)
Dash Tabasco
1½ teaspoons Old Bay seasoning
2 cups unsalted cracker crumbs
¼ cup vegetable oil

Cut the salmon into thirds. Bring about a quart of water to boil in a medium saucepan, then reduce the heat to low. Add the fish and poach, covered, for about 7 to 10 minutes until cooked through; drain, and place the fish in a medium bowl. Crumble, removing any bones.

In a large bowl, lightly beat the eggs and the milk. With a wooden spoon, stir in the mayonnaise, mustard, salt, pepper, parsley, scallions, Tabasco, Old Bay seasoning, and 1½ cups of the cracker crumbs. Add the fish and combine well. Cover with plastic wrap and refrigerate for 1 hour, or overnight.

In a large nonstick skillet set over medium heat, heat 2 tablespoons of the oil. Shape the salmon mixture into 2½-inch patties about 1 inch thick, and dredge them in the remaining cracker crumbs. Sauté the patties on both sides until browned, about 5 minutes per side. Serve warm or at room temperature.

(You can cook these the morning of your party and refrigerate them. Take them out of the refrigerator at least 2 hours before serving to allow them to come to room temperature, or warm them in a 300° F oven for about 10 minutes.)

Couscous with Vegetables and Dried Cranberries

Serves 8 generously

Using chicken stock instead of water enriches the flavor of this couscous salad. For a vegetarian version, use water or vegetable broth, and adjust the seasonings to suit your taste. The dried cranberries add a little something special, but you can substitute raisins if the cranberries are not available.

8 cups chicken stock
¼ cup extra-virgin olive oil
1 tablespoon salt, or to taste
1 teaspoon turmeric
¼ teaspoon cinnamon
½ teaspoon ground ginger
4½ cups uncooked couscous
1 cup dried cranberries
2 medium carrots, peeled and finely grated
2 medium zucchini, trimmed and finely chopped
½ medium red onion, finely chopped
1 large tomato, seeded and chopped
½ cup chopped cilantro
2 tablespoons fresh lemon juice
Salt
Freshly ground black pepper

Put the chicken stock, oil, salt, turmeric, cinnamon, and ginger in a large pot and bring to a boil. Gradually stir in the couscous and cook over medium heat until all the liquid is absorbed, about 5 minutes. Remove from the heat, cover, and let stand 5 minutes. Stir in the dried cranberries and grated carrots, cover, and let stand 10 minutes more.

In a large bowl, combine the zucchini, onion, tomato, and cilantro. Stir in the couscous, and sprinkle with the lemon juice. Add salt and pepper to taste.

(This can be made the day before. Remove the couscous from the refrigerator 2 hours before serving so it will come to room temperature.)

Bitter-Greens Salad

Serves 8

These richly flavored cheeses and bitter dark greens are good partners. Because the dressing is so simple, the distinct flavors of the salad really come through.

2 small heads escarole
2 heads romaine lettuce
2 bunches arugula
2 ounces Parmigiano Reggiano, slivered
6 ounces Gorgonzola cheese, crumbled
4 1-inch-thick slices fresh white peasant-type bread
2 large garlic cloves, peeled and halved
¾ cup extra-virgin olive oil
¼ cup red-wine vinegar
½ teaspoon salt
½ teaspoon freshly ground black pepper

Remove and discard the tough outer leaves and any bruised leaves from the escarole and romaine. Trim the stems from the arugula. Wash the greens, dry them well, and tear them into bite-sized pieces. Place the greens in a serving bowl and top with the Parmesan and Gorgonzola cheeses.

Lightly toast or grill the bread until it is warm but not browned. Rub the slices with the cut ends of the garlic cloves and cut the bread into 1-inch cubes. Sprinkle the croutons on top of the salad.

In a small bowl, mix the olive oil and vinegar, and add salt and pepper to taste; drizzle the dressing over the salad.

(Wash, dry, and tear the greens the morning of the party and keep them in a plastic bag in the refrigerator. Add some paper towels to the plastic bag to keep the greens from becoming soggy. The vinaigrette and cheeses can be prepared a few hours in advance and refrigerated as well.)

Chocolate-Pepper Hearts

Makes about 24 3-inch hearts

This recipe is adapted from *Martha Stewart's Weddings*. The taste of these cookies is initially sweet and chocolaty with a hot finish.

¾ cup (1½ sticks) unsalted butter, at room temperature
¾ cup granulated sugar
2 tablespoons light-brown sugar, packed
1 large egg, lightly beaten
1½ cups unbleached flour
¾ cup Dutch-process cocoa (sift cocoa before measuring)
Dash salt
1 teaspoon freshly ground black pepper
⅛ teaspoon cayenne pepper
½ teaspoon ground cloves

In the bowl of an electric mixer, cream the butter and the sugars on medium speed for 3 minutes. Beat in the egg, then add the flour, cocoa, salt, pepper, cayenne, and cloves, and mix well. Remove the dough from the bowl and shape it into a disc about 1 inch thick. Cover with plastic wrap and refrigerate for 1 to 1½ hours until disc is firm.

Preheat the oven to 325° F. Line a baking sheet with parchment paper and coat with vegetable-oil cooking spray.

Roll out the dough on a lightly floured board about ⅛-inch thick. Cut out the dough with a 3-inch heart-shaped cookie cutter. Place the cookies on the prepared sheet and bake for 10 to 15 minutes. Cool on a rack.

(These cookies can be made up to a month in advance and frozen.)

Lemon-Walnut Squares

**Makes 16 2½-inch squares or
32 1¼ × 2½-inch rectangles**

Everyone loves these lemon squares—the walnuts add an unexpected texture and rich taste. These are on the soft and delicate side, so try not to handle them too much.

¼ pound (1 stick) unsalted butter, softened
¼ cup confectioners' sugar
1 cup unbleached flour
½ cup chopped walnuts

2 large eggs, at room temperature
1 cup granulated sugar
3 tablespoons fresh lemon juice
1 tablespoon lemon zest
¼ teaspoon baking powder
1½ teaspoons flour
¾ cup chopped walnuts
Confectioners' sugar

Preheat the oven to 325° F. Spray a 10-inch or 11-inch square cake pan with vegetable-oil cooking spray and set aside.

First, make the crust: In the bowl of a food processor fitted with the metal blade, combine the butter and the confectioners' sugar and process until fluffy, about 1 minute. Add the flour and the walnuts, and process until smooth, 1 to 2 minutes. Remove the dough, press it into the prepared pan, and bake for 15 to 20 minutes until it looks light gold in color.

Meanwhile, make the lemon filling: In the bowl of an electric mixer, beat the eggs with the sugar on high speed until pale yellow and thick, about 5 minutes. Beat in the lemon juice, lemon zest, baking powder, and flour. Stir in the chopped walnuts with a wooden spoon.

Pour the lemon filling over the crust and bake for another 25 to 30 minutes, or until it looks set. Remove to a rack and let cool completely before cutting into 2- to 2½-inch squares. Just before serving, sift confectioners' sugar over the squares.

(You can make these up to 1 month ahead and freeze them.)

Intoxicating Fruit

Serves 8

The melon liqueur (like Midori, for example) brings out the flavor of the fruits, and its sweet scent is intoxicating. Vary the fruits depending on what is in season, but avoid using hard fruits like apples and pears.

2 pints strawberries
4 kiwis
1 small cantaloupe
1 small honeydew melon
3 tablespoons sugar
½ cup whole fresh mint leaves
¼ cup melon liqueur
1 tablespoon fresh lemon juice

Clean the strawberries and cut them in half. Peel the kiwis and cut them crosswise into ½-inch slices. Remove the rinds and seeds from the cantaloupe and honeydew and cut the flesh into 1-inch cubes. Place all the fruit in a large bowl and sprinkle with the sugar and the mint leaves.

In a small bowl, whisk together the melon liqueur and the lemon juice. Pour this over the fruit and toss it gently with your hands or a rubber spatula until it is well coated. (Be careful not to overhandle, because the fruit is delicate.)

(You can prepare the fruit in the morning, storing each in a separate bowl covered with a plastic wrap in the refrigerator. Add the other ingredients up to 3 hours before serving and keep refrigerated. Take the fruit out of the refrigerator 30 minutes before serving.)

Index